THE OPTION

THE OPTION

a memoir of suicide, mystery, and finding our way

Karin Stahl

2016

First Printing: 2016
ISBN-13: 978-1536842371

Cover art by John Beck

Praise for THE OPTION

THE OPTION made me weep. Karin Stahl has written a wise and lucid book about the most essential lesson of all: how – in the face of the incomprehensible – to go on.

Dani Shapiro, *Still Writing*

THE OPTION stares at unimaginable loss and doesn't blink. In unsparing prose, Karin Stahl's memoir articulates what it's like to live through a shocking, devastating loss--the operative words here are "live through," because despite everything, Stahl has managed to persevere and share her story with fierceness, determination, and clarity. In facing our own tragedies, we'd be lucky to have her gifts.

Mira Bartok, *The Memory Palace*

Karin Stahl writes with searing honesty, sorrow, and hard-won insight. Ultimately, her painful journey will serve as a beacon of hope – for other mothers, for their children, and for readers everywhere.

Jennifer Finney Boylan, *She's Not There*

I love this book for being a mother's book, for being excruciatingly honest, while also being – in the way I think mothers are – sometimes blind to things readers will not be blind to. That is part of the strength of the book. Instead, we are watching a woman in the process of trying to digest a story that never can be completely taken in.

Debra Spark, *Unknown Caller*

Karin Stahl's memoir is a heartfelt and beautifully written account about the unthinkable: What do we do when the worst possible thing happens to us, and how do we go on? As someone whose family endured its own tragedy, I greatly admire her honesty as well as her courage in sharing her journey. Her deep and abiding love for her daughter Kristina shines through on every page, even in the darkest moments, and reminds us that although we may not think it, we can survive.

Patrick Tobin, Screenwriter, *Cake*

A unique gift of reality, a part of life, which the writer permits outsiders to share. She guides us through a tunnel of darkness, which most people, especially mothers, attempt to suppress. It is impossible to remain merely an onlooker, as we penetrate the shadow, absorbing every step and thought, becoming one with the story. We cannot rest until she has exposed her world to reclaim memory of her lost daughter. Then will she achieve peace.   Irene Levin Berman, *Norway Wasn't Too Small*

Karin Stahl's memoir THE OPTION takes us to a heartbreaking place, to a loss that is unimaginable: the death of a child by suicide. Her words resonate with emotion as she leads us on a journey through intense grief allowing us to bear witness to the love that endures. Beautifully written, her honest account is a poignant reflection, a tender and intimate portrayal, of a family in their darkest hour.

D.D. Wood, *Songs for the Red King*

THE OPTION is a very powerful work … very moving. Many will find it helpful and eye-opening.

David F. Tolin, PhD, ABPP, *Face Your Fears*
Anxiety Disorders Center, Institute of Living, Hartford, CT

For Kristina and Bill

1

The line of mourners winds around the funeral home and there is a two-hour wait to move inside. More than seven hundred people have journeyed here, with more arriving all the time. As we drive into the back parking lot I see friends and students standing on the sidewalk, chatting together in low tones.

Police officers wave cars through the intersection. West Hartford is busy this Saturday evening. Outdoor patio seating at restaurants is already filling up. Light laughter blends with street noises and cheerful sounds carry in the warm autumn air.

A local TV station van, sniffing for news, stops in front of Molloy Funeral Home. "Who's died? Somebody famous? Look at all these people. Who was he?"

One of the policemen directs the van to move along, saying, "She was a local, a teacher, I think."

I hear a young girl in line mumble, "Idiot." I wonder what our daughter, Kristina, would think about the remark. Knowing her, she'd probably tell him that one day a woman will be President. How's that for news?

My husband, Bill, and I hesitate near our car, tempted to just stay outside in the early evening sunshine and avoid the brokenness within. After all, we are a parent's worst nightmare. We've lost our only child. Maybe one of the police will announce, "It's all a mistake. Go on home." Sure he will, for this cannot really be happening; lining up for calling hours feels unreal.

But no announcement comes. The cops wave cars on, the line creeps forward, and the vagary dies out.

Kingswood Oxford School (KO) in West Hartford arranged telephone calls to Kristina's closest students, advisees, and soccer team players. She was beginning her fourth year teaching there. The nation was in mourning the day she died, September 11, 2002, remembering the terrorist tragedies one year earlier in New York, Pennsylvania and Washington, DC. Later, the school community will wonder how much 9/11 influenced her decision to end her own life, but first they respond to the immediate tragedy and plan what to do for the students, faculty, parents and the public.

Before we left for the calling hours I dressed carefully. Not a vain careful. It was a one-button-at-a-time concentration, a grief careful. My actions had no urgency. For once I was not hurrying to get dressed, go out the door. After all, the worst had already happened. No rushing would bring our daughter back.

Just before the funeral home opens the doors, we see her for the first time since she died. She's in the coffin. Until that moment I didn't realize I needed to touch her and feel deeply in my mother hands that she really is dead.

The casket seems so big, much too large for her slender body. I gulp down the shock and tell myself this isn't Kristina. She's no longer really here. I touch her cold face in a caress, then put on her favorite silver and blue earrings. Bill stands beside me as I encircle Kristina's neck with a pearl necklace, a gift from him when she was sixteen. I add a second necklace her Colby lacrosse coach gave her as a senior that she wore all the time. Her neck is surprisingly unmarked or bruised.

Chris, her boyfriend, approaches the casket to include a Build-a-Bear they made together at the mall. There is a sweet dreams message in its paw that he recorded for Kristina to squeeze and play for nights apart.

They open the doors for the calling hours at five and the line moves steadily. Inside, our daughter's students and team players she coached seem small and forlorn in these surroundings of mourning and discreet lighting. We'd brought along CDs, music she played in her office at school, thinking the familiar sounds would be comforting. Numb with loss, the young people quietly inch forward toward us. They hold onto each other for support, gripping hands and standing stiffly. Awkward hugs. Shuffling feet. Some are by the walls, choosing distance as a shield. They look to the end of the line where we stand near the open casket. Eyes widen and they glance away. There is shock on some of their faces as they realize they are actually seeing her.

Many teachers are here, former colleagues and friends. They keep watch over their charges, ready to help with a kind word, a hug, and reassurances. It has been a long week for everyone. Wednesday, the day she died, the teachers broke the news of Kristina's suicide to advisees in homeroom. Then they stayed long after school ended each day to talk with students and provide comfort. For some students this is their first personal experience with someone dying young. Only older people die, right? Certainly not a teacher, coach and advisor just twenty-five years old, so alive only days before.

"What do I say?" a young man asks softly. He's with several boys dressed in khakis, oxford shirts and ties, and one of her favorite advisees that I met on the sidelines of a game.

"Tell them you're sorry for their loss. Offer to shake hands. If you remember something you liked about Ms. Stahl, go ahead and share that. Her parents want to know," answers the teacher.

Another student says in a shaky voice, "I'm afraid to see her."

"We're all here together. She'll look like she's sleeping."

"Why did she do it? What was so awful about her life?" I hold my breath, wondering what the teacher will say.

The teacher replies carefully, "We're all asking why. Think about it this way: she had a mental condition. We didn't even know. It got worse. Maybe the pain just got to be too much." The young student nods and then is quiet, thinking about it.

There are many similar conversations. Details of Kristina's suicide are not widespread yet. The newspaper reported only that she died in her home. I hear a few whispers at the entrance to the receiving room. No car accident then. *No illness. No violence from an intruder. Suicide? Not her. Maybe someone broke in, forced her to write a note, and made it look like a suicide?* Another vagary. In the wake of Kristina's death, myriad others look for any scrap of understanding.

My long-time friend and former college roommate is here. Pam is a talented poet and writing instructor at the University of Pittsburgh. She had just met Kristina for the first time this summer when we both traveled to the Bread Loaf School of English, Middlebury College, in Vermont where Kristina was pursuing her masters. As I hug Pam in the receiving line I remember vividly our last time together, the three of us.

"How could that beautiful, gifted, poised, loving woman I met, harbor inside her another self, unhappy enough to choose death over life?"

We stare at the casket. Kristina looks as if she is sleeping and might wake up at any moment to say, *What have I done? All these people ... I made a mistake. I want to come back, be a writer.*

The line keeps moving up to us by the casket. People share remembrances as we hug and weep together. Perhaps that is where the term calling hours comes from, the calling up of good times during these hours together.

"I remember Kristina from when we were all out at Red Oak Hill swimming, playing tennis and picnicking in the grove," says one family friend.

"She was always so happy. And that smile!" Other friends standing in line smile too, letting the good memories come.

Her former town league soccer coach shares a remembrance. "She was like a heat-seeking missile. Never saw such concentration, such focus. She was determined. *Mine*, she'd say. Then we'd watch her speed kick in. People used to stand up and cheer when Kristina took the ball."

Her travel soccer coach is next in line. "I remember when we won the state championship. Two overtimes. The rain was awful. Kristina played defense. No one could get by her. Not ever. The game was won in penalty kicks." I listen and wonder where her courage and drive were when she needed them.

The line continues on and on; people keep passing the casket. Photos sit on every surface around the room – childhood, high school, college, sports, family and vacations – heartwarming, happy times. A lacrosse stick by the edge of her bier is still wrapped with blue grip, ready for play. Students and parents have their arms about each other as they near us. Protective eyes seem to plead, "Be careful what you say to my daughter or my son."

Somehow Bill and I find the words. I feel blessed they are all here and I'm surprised, almost as a detached observer, at how long Bill and I stand. For four hours we greet, give and receive words of comfort with Kristina's students, players and friends.

Some of what I say is very deliberate and I concentrate to make my words as healing as possible:

"Try to think of all the good things you shared together, not her death."

"If you ever feel alone with a problem, tell your parents, your teachers, or an adult you trust. Ask for help."

"Thank you for coming. It means so much to us."

"Each day, ask your children what they are *feeling*. Really listen ... and then ... *ask them again*."

"She loved you too, talked about you all the time."

"Of course you're angry. She left you."

"We don't understand all this yet. Give yourself time."

"You regret your last words, sorry for how you left things? Believe that she knows. It's all right."

"No, suicide is not okay – it's not a solution. She simply couldn't go on."

A college friend of Kristina's greets another young woman joining the end of the line. "Hi, does anyone know what really happened? Among all our soccer players Stahlzie would be my last pick to kill herself."

"Her friend, Schieby, got one of Kristina's last emails. Sounded like she was dealing with a few things, but nothing *that* big."

"So, was she seeing a doctor?" asks another college friend who hadn't spoken to Kristina in a while.

"She saw a therapist for anxiety these last couple of years. Said she was doing better now," a Massachusetts friend adds.

"Well ... I wish she'd called one of us. Remember when she had panic attacks in the dorm? She always came to one of us then. Didn't she do anything, tell her parents, talk to her boyfriend, something?" No one answers.

We glean little bits and pieces – a few clues to her mental state, a couple of observations – picking at the mystery.

Kristina's favorite teacher has been waiting patiently with his wife, Carol. Bob Googins graciously offered to share his faculty office with Kristina when she first started teaching and there was a shortage of rooms. She was a former student of his and told us how wonderful he was to help her at school. I sink into their compassionate hugs. Hard to believe but two years from now they too will experience the loss of their daughter, also a teacher, to suicide.

One of Kristina's students and his father have been waiting in line for almost three hours to finally join us by the casket. The student is holding a copy of the Introduction page to his first published book, *The Firefighting Buff's Guide to New York City*. In it he thanks "my English teacher during my sophomore year of high school, Ms. Kristina Stahl, who taught me more about writing and the propriety of it than in all my previous years of school."

There is a swell of voices. Roommates from senior year at Colby College come through the line together. They lived with Kristina in a rented house in Waterville, Maine, a cheerful lemon yellow colonial. They give Bill and me hugs, sob and smile at the same time. I feel a burst of energy and uplift with these beautiful young women, their expressive voices sharing details of their lives since graduation. We are reluctant to release them.

Classmates from both high school and college mingle as they wait in line. Many young men chat about her athleticism, remembering her success in sports, her rapport off the playing fields as well. She was a tri-Varsity Captain in her high school senior year for soccer, basketball, and lacrosse, then an All-American lacrosse player two years of college. They joke quietly, appreciatively, about her rigorous workouts in the gym, her competitiveness, her sense of humor, and love of sports.

Her Colby College friends who came to help us yesterday look especially tired; they'd made numerous phone calls to bear the sad news and they enlarged favorite photos for display inside the funeral home. Shannon, the friend who looks like she could be Kristina's twin, prepared a special scrapbook of team photos, a precious gift that our family and friends have been poring over for hours. Although we haven't said it directly, we scan the pictures intently, looking at every expression on Kristina's face, every nonverbal posture, searching for anything resembling depression or unhappiness. So far we see only what we've always seen, a happy smile, warm embraces, closeness to friends, and her playful nature shining through. She seems happy with these wonderful teammates. They promise us, "We will be your daughters now."

"Mrs. Stahl, Kristina helped save my life," says a lovely brown-haired young woman. "She talked me out of suicide, got me to get help one night when I was giving up. Why didn't she call me? I called *her*." Her anguish is palpable as I hug her. Another loss to suicide? None would have guessed the risk in her too.

"Kristina loved you. Maybe she wanted to protect you," I say. The suicide impulse must have come upon her so fast not to call this understanding friend. "She was crossing a line without knowing it was even there." The young woman nods and buries her face on my shoulder.

The traffic grows less congested outside. Many visitors exit the funeral home now. Two police officers remain; as they are leaving, one tells his partner, "Hey, I have two daughters myself. That's all I've been thinking about tonight. I've got to get home."

It might as well be lettered on her casket: ACHIEVEMENT DOES NOT PREVENT SUICIDE. We hope some of the parents in line, like the policeman, will return home to talk with their own children, to ask tough questions: What are you feeling? Have you or one of your friends ever thought about suicide?

The thick sweet smell of the huge flower arrangements begins to overwhelm me now after hours breathing in, breathing out, disciplining myself to stand and talk at the same time. Bill looks exhausted, drained in every way. Families who came together are walking down the hall toward the parking lot, talking about coming to the one o'clock memorial service tomorrow. Their voices fade.

The cloying air is making me sick, and my feet throb after standing so long. I look around, hobble over to a chair, and lower myself into the seat. I know the time is coming when they'll close her casket ... a firm, tight, click and then she'll be locked inside forever.

Bill and the funeral director walk toward me; a keening sound escapes me. For some reason, having her body in my sight in the same room seemed okay, provided an anchor, reassured me she is not dead yet, still mine and here, not gone.

"It's time," Bill says.

He looks pale and shaky. He is tall and has to bend over to help me out of the chair. My feet hurt so much I have trouble walking even a few feet over to the casket. I see her, push back a strand of hair from her lovely face. Her freckles stand out on clear pale skin. So beautiful. I pat her arms gently, an automatic caress from years of mothering, and lean in to kiss Kristina one more time. I step back and grip Bill's hand as they close the lid, glad he has hold of me because immediately I want to open the casket again and never let her go.

We walk away, never to come back together after this absence. I feel I am abandoning her.

Calling hours end.

2

Before I learned of Kristina's death, I was at work that Wednesday. My office at Kaiser Permanente is spacious, with a row of windows looking out onto a magnificent magnolia tree. There is a round table for meetings, bookcases along one wall, a desk and counter, art on the walls, photographs of Bill and Kristina, and the usual marketing and sales plaques. Like Kristina, I keep a player and stacks of CDs. "Your nest," she called it. "I make a nest away from home too. Nice, huh?"

The Kaiser National Accounts health benefits sales and service team I joined three years ago includes fourteen experienced members. We have an exceptional rapport, somewhat unusual in sales, springing from a dedication to our customers, the company, and to the team's success as a whole, a competitive focus directed at rival companies, not each other. There was a wonderful CEO of the organization at the time, Dr. David Lawrence. He has an equally wonderful daughter, Jennifer, who was captain of Kristina's Colby College Women's Soccer team a few years ago. Bill and I met Dr. Lawrence on the sidelines of the soccer field one brisk Maine afternoon. His presence and conversation about Kaiser Permanente moved me and I found myself making a career change in 1998 to become part of the new National Accounts office being set up in the Northeast.

Diane, the assistant to our Senior Vice President, pokes her head around the corner and I smile.

"Hi, Karin. There's someone here to see you," says Diane.

I look up and see our minister from the Asylum Hill Congregational Church in Hartford, the Reverend Gary Miller. As soon as I see him I know something awful has happened, otherwise, why would he be here? I stand up quickly, almost tipping over the chair.

"What's happened?" I ask. I'm shaking already and dreading his answer.

"Why don't you come with me into the conference room?" Gary asks gently. *Okay, this is really going to be bad,* I think, *really, really bad.* Diane helps guide me out of the office and across the hall toward the closed conference room door. I see a few concerned faces of the team members looking over their cubicles as I pass by. The closed door is another bad sign. I walk slowly, feeling if I don't go in there that somehow, whatever it is, has not happened, not yet. Gary opens the door to the conference room. I glance to my right and see two people I do not recognize, a man and a woman. They look about mid-thirties, no greeting, no suits.

I glance to my left and see Bill. My relief is enormous. No auto accident. He is safe and here. Kristina is at school. Somehow I don't even think our child has been hurt. That's just not possible, so I turn as Gary takes my arm to guide me to the chair next to Bill on this side of the table.

"Karin, we have some bad news."

I ask, dreading the one word that will make it so, "Kristina?" I look at Bill, his eyes full of tears. He is unable to say anything. He nods. I jerk my head back to Gary.

"Kristina died this morning."

I clutch myself and feel like I am being split in two, so sudden and deep the pain. I bend over and grab the edge of the table. Gary puts a chair behind me and I sink into it. The team tells me later that I screamed a cry they recognized as a mother's wail from deep inside of me, full of terror and shock.

"How? Was she in a car accident?" I scan Gary's face.

"No ... She took her own life," Gary says softly.

"Oh, honey – oh no, no, no." I reach for Bill's hand, groping through my tears for my husband, her father, the only thing I recognize as stable in the room. Gary passes us tissues.

I glance up at the two strangers in the room, professionals looking at me with both compassion and suspicion. I know now why they are here. Gary introduces them as a detective and officer from the Farmington police force. They had responded to the 911 call.

"How did she die?" I ask them.

"She was found hanging," the male detective responds.

Hanging. There's no shielding my mind; it immediately creates an image of Kristina hanging, probably from the balcony in her living room. I snap back with shock. I feel horrified to think of her dying violently and alone. It doesn't sound like something Kristina could do to herself. Those thoughts are about all I allow for now. Time will come when I wrestle with images of her final moments, ones that I create and embellish in excruciating detail over and over in my dreams.

That's that then. All hope flees. I try to get my mind around this event that completely changes our world.

Bill begins to talk to me and I nod, hearing how the officers notified him at Aetna and then he asked to contact Rev. Miller so he could accompany them when they told me. The police want to keep Bill – and now me – in their sights throughout these steps. I learn later this is standard procedure in the event the coroner finds evidence of foul play. At the time I have no idea our reactions are being carefully scrutinized.

The rest happens quickly. I am in too much shock to drive so the female officer takes my car and follows us back to our house. Bill, Gary and I drive in Bill's car and begin the first of many discussions surrounding Kristina's death and the aftermath of suicide. School colleagues and friends join us at home after Gary makes a few calls. Before beginning the awful task of speaking with our long distance family members, we talk and sort through the details of her last days, hours, and conversations for clues to Kristina's mental state at the time.

For several minutes, her school colleagues offer up pieces of the recent past to us, ideas they think may have depleted Kristina's reserves. We are like trackers casting back on a trail, trying to find out how her well ran dry. Bewilderment and pain infuse her boyfriend's words. Chris has a gentle Southern cadence when he speaks.

"We promised each other we'd always be honest. How could she not tell me what she was feeling? She sounded discouraged the last phone call we had Tuesday night but it didn't seem like a life crisis."

Then it's my turn to recount what I remember about my last telephone conversation with her, an hour before the call she made to Chris, remarkably consistent with his.

"Just like yours. She even used the same phrases. I completely missed the signs, never thought she was depressed or suicidal. I thought we were just solving a teaching problem together. Those were the last words I heard Kristina speak," I recall.

Saying that makes me dizzy. I have an immediate urge to jump up and see if we have any recordings of her voice in the house. I want to play back messages on the answering machine and I'm worried that I probably deleted them since she leaves us so many during a normal week. I need to hear her voice. I feel frantic, fixated on this small thing, being able to hear her voice.

The Head of School, Lee Levison, is here at the house too, along with the school counselor. Lee shares what he learned from Kristina's department supervisor, Ron Monroe, and a few others at school. He tells us about one student who complained about Kristina's expectations, thought they were too high, didn't like her "stupid performance agreement" for the students and parents. Apparently he challenged her verbally in class after not completing his homework three days in a row saying, "Go ahead and call my parents."

Kristina's supervisor overheard the student and his friend talking at the copier, so Ron checked with Kristina to see if she needed any help. Then he let the department head know. They both thought it didn't seem like a big deal at the time.

Sunday night before she died, Kristina told us she felt embarrassed that Ms. Hanson, the department head, was informed too, even though they reassured her they support her work and judgment in the classroom. They wanted to be helpful. "On a scale of one to ten, this incident didn't even register as a problem," Dr. Levison tells the family and friends. Nevertheless, it is apparent from her last phone conversations that Kristina concluded she was failing as a teacher.

"A student misbehaving in class caused her suicide?" I'm having trouble grasping that. This was all about *homework*? Something else must have happened to make this a trigger for suicide. Feeling more anguish, I clutch my middle with a powerless sinking feeling. Fright pounds through me. I wonder if this is what her panic attacks felt like.

Finally, we look at each other with nothing more to share about Kristina's last days, last hours, last conversations, at least for this tragic afternoon. No conclusions. No certainties. Nothing more about her personal tipping point.

3

It is the day after Kristina's death. Like the day before, and the day before that one, the September weather is stunning with bright sunshine and warmth, yet I am cold, so cold. I'm in a fleece jacket huddled on the sofa in the living room, watching the sun rise and move above the tree line, nursing a big cup of coffee I don't remember fixing.

Last night Bill and I couldn't sleep. We lay in our bed holding each other through the shock and disbelief, talking in whispers and gasps, sobbing, and shaking in anguish. Just before dawn, I see he's finally fallen asleep and I quietly leave the bedroom with BC, one of our cats, who pads along beside me. I settle into a corner of the sofa, gazing out at the patio and back yard. BC climbs into my lap and begins purring. As I stroke him I cry again, tears dropping onto his fur.

After a while I get up for more coffee, sit back down. I keep sitting there, not moving, playing scenes of Kristina in my head, especially the last conversations and phone calls.

I never got to say good-bye, only good night. There's a difference. When she was little, after prayers we said good night and expected to see each other in the morning. When we ended our last phone call I remember saying, "I love you Kristina. Sleep tight and good night." Kristina said, "I love you. Thank you." She didn't say good-bye or good night.

Around ten o'clock, I hear a car outside on the gravel. My sister, Ginny, is arriving after her red-eye flight from California. I stand at the open front door and watch as she steps out of an airport taxi and looks up. Her light strawberry blonde hair moves in the September breeze. I take the two brick steps quickly, wrap her in my arms, and breathe her in with gratitude.

"I'm so glad you're here," I murmur and then immediately start crying. We hold each other and hear a car door shut. The cab pulls away, climbs the drive. Then we're left with morning birds chirping, a dog barking down the street, and the sound of BC meowing from the open door. Ginny draws back to look at me.

"The boys and their Amys will be coming tomorrow. They had some things to do first." She is referring to her three sons; two are married to women named Amy.

"That means so much," I say. The gathering is beginning now and I'm grateful. My brother, Rik, said he's left phone messages on his daughter Erika's cell. "Erika and Nick are in Block Island, Massachusetts, on vacation. They may come on Sunday. Aunt Joann and Gary are driving from Pittsburgh and Ann will come from Vermont."

"I haven't seen so much family since Mother and Dad died," her voice trails off. She walks up the steps beside me, stoops to pick up and hug our cat. With her blue eyes, freckles, slender and strong build, my younger sister's can-do attitude conquers projects I would never attempt. She just keeps going like the furry drum-beating rabbit in TV commercials, a good companion for the next difficult tasks.

After an hour's rest and breakfast, Ginny and I leave for Kristina's condominium to pick out burial clothes. Bill remains back at home making calls, waiting for the police to come by and release Kristina's good-bye note left for us.

"Did the police tell you anything about what the condo looks like?"

"Yes. There isn't much. Police left everything the way it was yesterday morning when Chris found her."

"Her boyfriend?" Ginny asks. I nod yes.

"He teaches at the school too. When she didn't show up for homeroom or her first class, he offered to drive over and check on her."

I pause, trying to concentrate and remember what Chris told us yesterday afternoon when we were all together sharing what we knew. "Kristina called Chris after me that night. Her last conversation was with him. He said she sounded discouraged, tired, but he didn't pick up on anything threatening."

Chris has his own key and had come in when there was no answer to the doorbell. The shock of discovery was horrifying and traumatic. He called 911 and stayed outside on the walkway until the police arrived. After securing the site and removing her body around noon, the police went to meet with Bill at his office in Hartford.

"They said it was no accident, no sign of foul play, note left behind; the coroner ruled it a suicide." I choke on those words, swipe at my running nose, and grip the steering wheel. I probably shouldn't be driving, but it's only half a mile from our house on the same road, Talcott Notch. No commuter traffic at this time in the morning, hardly any cars driving through the woods with us.

I pull into my usual parking spot near the walkway leading to Kristina's front door. Turn off the car. Turn to Ginny. "Why didn't I feel something like a warning when she called the night before? I remember her saying she sometimes hated herself. She thought she was failing at teaching. Is that enough to kill yourself? Stupid me; I tried to *reason* with her, reminded her how wonderful her students and supervisor think she is. I'm her mother ... and I didn't help her."

I bend over the wheel, sob and shake, hating the pain. Last night and in the early dawn I went over and over these same things, how I screwed up, missed the signs of her suicide.

"We talked about her classes, how students were reacting to a performance agreement for their parents to sign, how to handle one difficult student. Our call was all about her teaching. I didn't understand her feelings. She was desperate and giving up."

Ginny reaches over and rubs my shoulders lightly. "She told you only what she wanted to. She loved you. She was protecting you." That comment makes me shiver.

"Protecting me from what?"

"From her feelings, her anxiety. She may have already made her decision to die." That thought scares me. I shake, cold again. I search my sister's eyes and plead with her.

"But she always talked with us about things, her feelings, and problems. Why not feeling suicidal?" I shake my head. I know I need to talk about this more, but right now I'm spent. I am so tired I can hardly open the car door and step out.

Kristina's unit is between two corner ones. This section is private, shaded by trees in the courtyard. The rough vertical siding is classic 1970s, the units well kept, and the grounds are beautiful. Most walks are lined with pachysandra, rhododendron, hosta, and mountain laurel. Our footsteps are almost soundless on the smooth blue stones as we move in and out of shadows and sunlight. As we get closer to the front door, wind chimes offer up a few bell-like notes in the light breeze. I reach up to touch them, brushing my hand on the chimes as I usually did when I came to see her.

"This is so pretty," Ginny says. "It has a nice feel. Did she have friends here?" I'm about to put my key in the front door lock, then pause. Her question makes me think.

"Not really. She mentioned meeting her neighbors next door when she first moved in nine months ago. Then she was away so much this summer. That makes it hard to meet neighbors."

When Bill and I came daily to feed the cat, we didn't run into anyone either. Now I recall something Kristina mentioned, that she felt uneasy sometimes when she came home at night. There are a hundred units in the community and, although well-lit, her assigned parking garage is in a separate area, so she walked across the pavement and up the stairs that are dark and partially covered by branches.

"I know I'm being silly," Kristina told me. "Nothing's happened. There's hardly anyone around. I'm sure I'll get used to it. A few more months and it won't feel so strange."

This September morning the sun streams through the windows when Ginny and I walk inside. It is quiet and warm, a soothing feeling. It seems like Kristina just stepped out for an errand and will be coming back any minute. As we move into the entry hall her cat, Annabelle, rises and stretches from a nest by the slider that opens onto a patio and woodsy backyard. The slider spot is where Annabelle suns and keeps an eye out for chipmunks, squirrels and occasional deer. The fluffy white feline, one green eye, one blue, pads over to greet us and rolls onto her back, looking cute and appealing. Ginny bends over, hand outstretched.

"Careful," I caution. "She does that trick to con you into petting her. Then she scratches."

Poor Annabelle is a feral cat rescued from Boston, a cat we all say only Kristina could love, one that strikes fear in the hearts of Kristina's friends. No one knows when Annabelle will pounce, so I'm very respectful of the cat's space and no longer try to touch her when she chooses to brush against me, leap onto the arm of a chair I am sitting in, or follow me around. It's a stand-off when our daughter's away.

The townhouse is spacious. From the entry we walk into a living room directly in front of us. There is a cathedral ceiling. The upstairs hallway overlooks the living room and there are two bedrooms and a bath on the second floor. Off the living room there's a dining room that has a set of louvered café doors that open into a narrow kitchen. There is a small powder room next to the stairs. Chris added his skilled labor to paint blue in the kitchen, warm terra cotta in the dining area, shades of sage on most of the walls and stairwell. All of the rooms in her home reflect Kristina's cozy style. The comfortable sofa, chair and ottoman in the living room are brick red colored denim, trimmed in khaki piping. We see a cherry coffee table, end table, bookcases, stereo, CDs and phone.

A familiar quilt in autumn-toned sage and rust colors, the one she wrapped around herself in front of the fire, is now folded neatly on the back of the sofa. A woven woolen throw draped over the chair looks just like the gift she gave me in July. I stroke the soft yarn and remember her saying, "You should see this store in Middlebury where I got the throw for you. They have stacks of Irish weaves. I got one for me too, a little different green."

I sigh. Nothing looks *changed*. Nothing feels different or awful. Her home is warm and inviting, a sweet place full of her things, her cat, her scents.

The police warned us there would be evidence upstairs. I now deliberately look up from the living room to the solid half-wall balcony that runs the length of the upstairs hallway. I shiver and my eyes scan – looking for marks, trying to find the spot where she hanged herself. I start up the carpeted stairs, treading cautiously. The steps are narrow and there's a small landing halfway up. That's where I start shaking, stumble and grab the handrail to pull myself up the remaining steps, afraid of what I'll see.

There's a twisted blue-striped sheet stretched along the balcony floor. It extends from her bedroom and is still tied to the bedpost. I take it in, trying to figure it out. How did she know how to tie the sheets? There are half-empty bottles of Advil and Aleve, a few pills have escaped and lie there. Two of her water bottles sit on the bathroom sink counter, the kind athletes use with long bent tubes to squirt fluids into their mouths, old battered bottles we'd seen Kristina pack with her gear game after game. Now, each is partially filled with water, as if she'd taken the pills but changed method and moved into the bedroom for sheets to hang herself. Maybe she hesitated or thought about calling us while tying knots.

My knees give way. I kneel on the carpet and lean against the back wall, looking at the sheets and stray pills. There is a scene in front of me, absolute proof she constructed the means for her death here. I imagine the last few minutes of her life. She twists the bed sheets together, winds them around the leg at the foot of the bed, ties them. In my head I see her hold the loop made by the sheets and climb onto the solid balcony, then sit there to put the sheet noose over her head. Her hand holds the loop close to her neck as she pushes off strongly with closed eyes. The force of her fall ends her suffering quickly in my vision of her death. I choose crisp, impulsive, and final.

Compelled, I get up and slowly move to the edge of the balcony. I lean over, wondering what Kristina's last view was like. Suddenly, there is a piercing yowl. I glance down at the cat below me. Annabelle is directly underneath the balcony in the living room and she has a look of terror in her eyes, a trembling body, a fear I have never seen in an animal before. She cries again and I pull back. It's me, I realize. My sister races up the steps and comes over to my side.

"She must have seen it happen," I say to Ginny. She nods, agreeing with me. Poor Annabelle; I can imagine how awful it was to see the one special person in your life die, the only patient one who never gave up on loving a defensive cat. Neither of us leans over the balcony again. We walk into Kristina's bedroom, painted a cheery yellow. The bed is made up with a lavender poppy flower print comforter and pillows. It registers right away – *she didn't go to bed that night.*

"The furniture is new," Ginny comments. "Everything's beautiful."

"Kristina asked me to come along when she shopped," I tell her. The bedroom pieces are Shaker-style, painted sage green with oak tops and knobs. I run my hand over her dresser things: perfume bottles, jewelry chest, hand mirror, candle. Even now there is nothing out of place. "She was so proud of herself ... that she'd saved money. She didn't want her furniture to be a present from us."

"I have Pottery Barn taste on a Bob's Surplus budget," Kristina told me. She looked through dozens of catalogs then shopped for substitutes. I was impressed with how organized she was, how she knew just what she wanted and how she wanted to live with each piece. It was great fun going to the store together.

Ginny crosses the room and opens closet doors. "Oh, my ... " She's staring. There are very, very neat rows of slacks, tops, shoes and boots. All the trousers hang exactly the same way, facing the same direction. The blouses are sorted by color. Athletic clothes and gear are stored on the right side, school and dress clothes on the left. Built-in shelves have tidy occupants. Not a thing out of place, so perfect it is astonishing. During the time since Kristina moved into the condo she often talked about doing her housecleaning this weekend or that, happy to have her own place to decorate and keep up. At first I used to think she raced around tidying things up before I arrived. Then I began to think she never messes it up, like sleeping in place in a bed, not moving, so it's easier to make. Everything, even now, looked like an ad in a magazine.

"Not black," I whisper to my sister. "She wore black often for work, said it was practical at school. Her favorite color is blue." Ginny finds a blue and yellow sleeveless linen dress. It's new, never worn, one Kristina told me she bought as part of her new look for the academic year. "I'm going to try some more color. I'm saving it for a fall day when it's cooler," she grinned. Her last thank you note is a card with a dark haired girl on the front, holding a white cat.

My hands close now around her favorite pair of socks. "The students called these her Wicked Witch socks because of the broad red and black horizontal stripes. We'll definitely bury her in those," I tell Ginny.

I move to the neat closet, look through the stacks of shoes, and pull out red Danko clogs to add to the small pile on the bed. It is not possible we're choosing burial clothes. The annoyance feels so powerful, so strong I almost turn around and run away. Instead, I drop the socks on the bed and walk across the hall to the second bedroom, set up as a study. I sit on the small sofa, look at her writing desk. The sofa is actually a futon from her last apartment. We picked it out together at Pier 1 Imports, fit it into the back of her Jeep, and then hefted it together up narrow stairs, giggling most of the way. Sitting here feels good. Familiar.

There are books stacked neatly next to soccer clipboards. She's been coaching for three years. This would have been her fourth season. I see she's drawn out play diagrams, typed up drills, made notes on player rosters. She's done all this since coming back from graduate school where she spent most of the summer. She was in her second of five summer sessions at the Bread Loaf School, Middlebury College School of English in Vermont. The Master's degree program is well known and she was so proud of being selected. Robert Frost was associated with Bread Loaf. He was also a father who knew the loss of two children, one by suicide.

A memory comes to mind from when my friend, Pam, and I drove up to see Kristina on a gorgeous July morning just two months ago. We listened to a mix of oldies but goodies made for the road trip, both of us singing along. The plan was to see Kristina, go out to dinner together, stay overnight, then drive to Portland, Maine, for our annual reunion with a small group of college friends and sorority sisters. Kristina and I were excited about getting together beforehand and had been exchanging emails for days. "Finally, Mom! I'll get to meet your writer friend!" she wrote.

I daydream some more ... Kristina is greeting us outside the main building, dressed in her blue shorts and white t-shirt, carrying books, hurrying across the lawn from a class that just ended. I remember thinking how beautiful she is, a feeling I often have when we've been apart for a while. Her blues eyes and infectious grin embrace me. She doesn't seem embarrassed when I hug her tight, whisper mother things to my precious child, and then step back to introduce her to Pam.

We lunch by the river, shop, eat dinner at the lovely Waybury Inn, and then sit in on one of Kristina's classes the next day before leaving for Maine. I watched the beginning of a wonderful connection between two writers, saw them discuss books, authors, and their own writing projects. I was basking in the moment, enjoying the special evening and the glow that surrounded us.

I mentally shake myself back into the present as Ginny comes into the study. "Are you okay?"

"I think so ... just remembering." I get up and start back downstairs. Now that we found clothes I'm anxious to leave.

4

A few minutes after we arrive home, the police detective stops by to bring us Kristina's suicide note.

We recognize her handwriting. There are no smudges, cross outs, blotches from tears – nothing to indicate distress when she wrote it. There's no greeting or signature. She wrote:

> *I am so sorry for the trouble I caused. I am ashamed to think of what will happen tomorrow. But I hate myself too much. God, I am so sorry. I do not know what to do. I feel so alone and yet I know there are people who love me. Please forgive me. I cannot do this anymore. I know I will keep failing. I must find somewhere safe to be. Please forgive me. I love you. I will love you forever. I will love you forever. I am too selfish. I cannot forgive myself. Please forgive me. Please believe me. I am so ashamed.*

He tells us few suicides leave a letter, perhaps twenty percent of the time, so Bill and I are especially grateful for her courage to write. We want to understand what she was feeling at the time of her death, what may have caused her to kill herself and leave us all.

Although we will read her letter many times over the years ahead, share it with her doctor, family and friends, the very first understanding we gain is that even though Kristina knew she was loved, love was not enough to save her.

5

The kitchen counter supports me as I grip the edge with both hands outspread, feeling a sharp pain in my midsection. Up close, the cool white tiles feel good on my forehead. I breathe the same way I learned in childbirth classes, panting like a small animal being chased. It works. The ache recedes and I'm aware friends are here in the kitchen with me. It's lunch time, day two, and they've brought food. Soft pats soothe my shoulders and I loosen my grip.

"Breathe. That's it. You're okay."

Deb's steady nurse voice coaches me. Kristina babysat Deb's daughter years ago, but I can't remember what time she and Jim arrived from Canada today. Joan and Judy's faces come into focus now too. I squeeze my eyes shut to gulp air, then after a few moments I look up and see more friends looking on – Tess, Clare, Margaret, Donna and Debby. Not sure it's even the same day. Grief is funny that way, fast-forwarding you from scene to scene in jerks.

"I'm okay," I manage to reassure, swiping at my eyes. Clare passes me a tissue and I blow with relief. Margaret reaches for a glass of water and passes it across the counter to me.

"Thank you," I manage to say, then down the entire glass, enormous gulps as if I'd been parched for days. I recognize the signs of dehydration and wonder how long since I've had something to drink. The time span from when we heard about Kristina has been filled with caring people coming and going, phone calls, food appearing and disappearing. Yet I can't remember actually eating or drinking.

The phone rings and someone brings it to Bill in the next room. I hear gravel crunching, footsteps on the brick walk, the front door opening, low voices, and steps coming into the kitchen. Too much. I slide my head back onto the counter and close my eyes.

6

A coffin is not a choice for a child, not a decision we ever thought we'd be making for our daughter.

The funeral director has been exceptional, guiding us compassionately through the steps to have Kristina's body released from the coroner and a death certificate drawn up. The last call we had was when the director told us our daughter arrived and, for one insane moment, I didn't remember it is *her body*, not her. Her corpse (awful word) has traveled from the bowels of a state morgue following the autopsy process. It feels unusual being in the same building with Kristina, yet not feel her presence or any spark of life.

Bill's eyes are red and irritated from tears. I'm moving slowly, dreading the meeting. Ginny looks remarkably awake, no jet lag yet. As kind as everyone is being by bringing lunch, making calls, handling things back at the house while we make arrangements, this is exhausting, hard work. The pain slices again. I pant, breathe, and walk into the office.

There are few things memorable about any of the decisions regarding Kristina's obituary, accompanying photo, remembrance cards, guest books, and grave stone. But the coffin is another matter entirely. We are hoping to have an open casket for viewing at the calling hours. The underlying thought is, if she doesn't look bruised from the hanging, seeing her at peace will help provide closure for her students and young friends after such a sudden death.

The room of display coffins is large and overwhelming with casket samples lining the walls under bright lights. For some silly reason I recall one of Kristina's favorite Disney movies, *Pollyanna*, the part where the invalid, Mrs. Snow, is picking out her own casket lining. Choices,

choices. We look at cherry, mahogany, oak, pine, metal, and space-aged grey fiberglass; all to enclose our only child and then consign her to the ground. "What do you think Kristina would like?" we're asked.

"Definitely not metal or plastic," I answer. The mahogany looks too formal, the oak too busy.

"How about cherry wood, something warm?" That feels right to me. Ginny and Bill both nod, agreeing. Then we decide about the lid. Should it be full or only half-opened for the viewing?

"Half-open," I answer, surprisingly quickly. "This way we'll put Kristina's striped socks and clogs on her feet, have it be a private thing, separate from the dress people will see her wearing on the top half." Even in death I want to protect her from prying eyes, something she would hate. As I pass the red clogs, underwear, socks, and dress to Randy, I marvel that it was only two weeks ago she talked me into a pair of green clogs for myself. The mischief, the sharing, the utter sweetness of our time shopping together comes back ... "I wear my red ones all the time, Mom. You'll love them!" Kristina gushed at the time and I grinned, happy to see her smile. Most of that afternoon she had been quiet, preoccupied with school work. Now, we're preparing her for a grave.

7

"Karin ... Karin?" Bill is sitting next to me, touching my shoulder to get my attention. I don't remember the drive, yet I'm at the church now and sitting in our minister's office. Three worried faces. I start and sit up, reconnecting with the present moment. Our minister, Bill, Ginny and I are planning the memorial service. There are more choices about readings, scripture, music, hymns, and who to invite to speak at the memorial.

"Sorry," I say. "Just got lost for a minute."

What was it Kristina used to tell me when things got hectic, something she told herself? I remember. It was from another one of her favorite movies, "Home for the Holidays." Claire Danes tells Holly Hunter, her mother in the film, to relax, to remember the blowfish and "just float." I can hear Kristina's voice in my head – *just float.*

8

"You're not coming to Kristina's funeral?" Bill's voice is incredulous, upset. He's talking with his father, Ray, in Florida. Although he called him immediately after we had the news and the date for her service, we haven't heard from Ray about his travel arrangements yet.

"Son, I promised your mother."

"You promised her what?" Bill's voice is getting louder. "She has Alzheimer's, Dad. She doesn't even recognize you now."

"I know, but I made her a promise that she'd never be alone. That I'd never leave her."

"Dad, you have health aides around the clock for her. She won't be alone." Bill pauses, takes a breath. "This is your only grandchild. Mom would want you to be here. She won't even know if you're gone for two days." Bill sounds pleading. Long pause.

"I'd know," his father replies.

"But what about us?! I need you too, Dad. Karin's family is coming and there won't be any Stahls here for me." Silence. No response.

On the second phone line I'm holding my breath, trying not to interrupt their conversation, sensing Ray is digging in and won't be changing his mind. I am upset, shaking with enormous restraint. This grief-anger is so great I feel a growl about to burst from my throat.

If Bill were the one who had died, not Kristina, I wonder if Ray would come to his only son's funeral. He'd probably arrange a memorial service in Florida where his friends there would comfort him, separate from whatever I'd do in Hartford.

Ray has left his Connecticut home behind, us too it appears. Ironically, the reason we'd purchased the Stahl family plot in the Farmington Riverside Cemetery six months ago was because Bill's mother's health was failing and at that time she seemed near death, was moved into hospice care. She's now doing well physically but very poorly cognitively. Kristina, Bill and I visited his parents in June, only three months ago, and Anna Lou briefly recognized her granddaughter. The last memories they had of Kristina were happy caring ones. It's not fair, not normal for Kristina to die first.

"Are you not coming because she killed herself, because it was suicide?" Bill asks. Good for him, I think, push for the truth from your father. I'm quiet, taut as a piano string. No answer.

Bill's father is a lawyer and no stranger to using long pauses in his work. We've been through his manipulation before. Bill out-waits him. I hear movement on Ray's end through the phone and then he sighs.

"I'll send you some money from your mother and me for the reception. You know I'd be there if I could." Defeat. I know once Ray gets formal in his speech that means the end of whatever conversation we're having with him.

"Thank you, but money isn't necessary," Bill says each word carefully. He's really infuriated. As much as I love my father-in-law, my outrage right now is huge. I'm insulted he's trying to make amends with money because he's unwilling to take a three-hour plane trip in the off-season, returning practically before my mother-in-law wakes up from a nap. Tears start and I close my eyes, rigid with this awful anger.

Ray says, "I'll mail a check to you today. Give everyone our best. We love you." At this point I can't hold it in.

"Dad, some of your friends have called us. They said they'll look for you at the funeral. Of course, we expected you'd be here ... " I'm hoping he hears my hurt. I hate that he won't come when Bill needs him. I wish Ray could see his son's face, see how crushing this decision is for an only child losing *his* only child. Something more is breaking here. We say good-bye and hang up.

9

Cheers from the Kingswood Oxford vs. Miss Porter's girls' soccer game come from behind me as I kneel beside Kristina's grave two days after we laid her to rest at Riverside Cemetery. I had walked across the street from the soccer field during half time. A warm afternoon, barely a breeze, still summery feeling, and the grave is mounded with flowers, surprisingly beautiful and still fresh from the calling hours and memorial service. Bees buzz, alight on petals, and creep into the roses, lilies and sunflowers.

It was winter when we bought the plot. The grave overlooks the water. Canada geese swam in the stream and children were sledding on the hill behind the section where I kneel now in the sun. I'm grateful Kristina is buried here, close to home, near a school for girls and adjacent to an athletic field. We'll need this special spot for prayers and reflections, a place to be. If we had cremated her and scattered her ashes, I know my mother's soul would have scattered as well.

I've brought her some gifts. I hold her poem "Silent Warrior," written the first year of coaching the soccer team. I also have a black and white armband. The team honored their former assistant coach by wearing bands with "Silent Warrior 23" on them. A favorite player, Diane, had made each one by hand the night before. Her face was one of the first we spotted on the crowded field as she hurried over to greet us and put on the band before the game started.

"We are so glad you came today," she said and gave us a hug. Several players spotted us after Diane ran back onto the field to warm up. Laura's bright red hair cheered us. Sara gave a small wave.

"Oh, Bill ... this hurts." I turn to him on the slight rise overlooking the field and bury my head in his shoulder, wishing I could hide out.

27

Other parents then join us on the grass.

Kneeling beside the fresh grave now, I talk out loud to Kristina. "Hi, sweetie. Just saying hello. You'd be proud of the team; they're ahead at the half. Laura and Shea told me they're scoring for you today especially. Diane is playing well too. She made all the arm bands. Here's yours ... and they gave your poem to everyone at the game today. We all miss you. Bye for now. I'll be back soon." I place her arm band and poem on top of the flowers, bend over and smell the closest rose.

Silent Warrior

A commitment to a team takes courage. Not the kind of courage it takes to run through the exhaustion or a stomach cramp, or the rain and the blazing heat of the late summer months, though that too is something to be proud of. A commitment to a team takes the courage of a silent warrior, the silent hero who does not work for the award or the win or the cheers from a crowd. The silent warrior battles her self; she challenges herself when no one is looking, when no one thinks she is working. She asks for nothing and assumes everything. She trusts herself and her teammates without doubt. She knows that what effort she gives is what effort others give too. She is not alone but standing on a green field of other warriors, waiting, silently, for the real game to begin.

Kristina Stahl, October 15, 2000

10

It is impossible to guess how many road trips we three have been on together over the years since Kristina began soccer. By sixteen she had a lean and strong 5'7" frame. Her hair was dark brown and worn in a long ponytail for the games. When Kristina competed she brought a focus and intensity to soccer that made her coaches proud. They knew Kristina simply did not stop or give up.

It was exciting watching her. She was a left-footed, highly strategic player who made speed her friend. We'd see her scan the field, eyes narrowing as she picked out players here and there among the opponents whose style of play she'd assess, decide where a vulnerability was, and pass on the information to her teammates. They shared some of Kristina's commentaries on the sidelines that would go like this:

"Amy said Kristina has spotted #11's weakness. She always veers to the left around an attacker."

"Glad she told Megan to run right side around #3. She made that last goal. How'd she know that?"

How indeed? Kristina had a sense of the play, anticipated what an opponent would probably do, something she gained by studying and watching. She was an observer on the sidelines for a year before starting to play herself.

"Do you want to sign up for town soccer today? The West Hartford league has tryouts for nine-year-olds," I suggest.

"No. I want to play when I'm ten."

"Any particular reason, honey?" I ask.

"I'll be better then. I don't want to make mistakes."

"It's all right to make mistakes, you know. We all do."

She looks at me again, "Well, I want to wait and do my best."

Bill and I agree not to push Kristina into anything. Our thought is she will learn to pace herself without our programming every step. Besides, there's too much pressure already and we want her to enjoy childhood. So, for a year she stays on the sidelines, concentrating on the game intently as if videotaping it for playback in her head. One morning at breakfast she tells us, "I'm ready to sign up for soccer now." Just like that, the year of watching is over.

"Kristina is very fast," her first coach says. "We don't know whether she should be a forward or play defense, so we may be having her play a few positions to find out."

This coach is known for his excellent patient style, a gentle way that is spot on with the players, bringing out their best. Once Kristina's first game begins, the players seem impossibly tiny out there in over-sized uniforms. Little girls stop whatever they're doing to hike up shorts, kneel to tie shoelaces on cleats, or tuck in long shirts. Sometimes they whirl around, losing sight of the other players and the ball. The most frequent coaching is, "Watch the ball!"

Our eyes never leave Kristina. We see her hunker down in what the coach terms "a natural defensive posture." She looks wound up, ready to accelerate, a stance she never loses as she plays through her high school and college years, eventually coaching teams. It's as if Kristina has another gear. We can almost hear her revving up and shifting.

"That was just perfect," a parent says next to us. "Quite a daughter you have there."

Now, after her death, I realize perfect isn't a compliment; it's the beginning of expectations and anxiety about always doing things just right. Only injuries stop her.

The goalies love her. They know with Kristina in the backfield she'll keep the line strong and prevent shots on goal. When she takes the ball she runs so fast the other team players are still turning around by the time she is mid-field. Most opposing team coaches double-team her and it is not uncommon to see multiple substitutions for the players covering Kristina, while she is rarely off the field.

During a drive down the left side her face tightens up, her eyes narrow slightly and our smiling girl looks ready to do battle. She simply never stops, never lets down, always feels driven to play her best. She goes to a private place during competition. Her focus is daunting and unrelenting. A silent warrior.

11

Bill and I have an appointment with Kristina's therapist, Dr. K, two days after the memorial service. The doctor and I met briefly during the funeral reception and her words surprised me.

"Kristina didn't talk about her athletic skills," she said. "This service explains some things."

During the memorial, the Colby Women's Soccer and Lacrosse teams lined up in front near the pulpit. A few young women took turns speaking about Kristina's skills, her commitment as a player, leadership, warm sense of humor, and her love for them. Two coaches spoke too, sharing with us what they had seen in Kristina's athletic focus and concentration, an intensity and quality of play that raised her above the norm as a defensive strategist.

I assumed Dr. K was commenting on Kristina's modesty, not bragging about her athleticism in the therapy sessions, but I am wrong. Dr. K had been undecided before the service, guarding Kristina's medical background as an adult patient, not certain of us or our motives for requesting a meeting. When we asked her for an appointment after the service, she said, "I'll meet with you this week."

Bill and I join her now, walking into the same red brick West Hartford office where Kristina had her sessions. We bring a copy of Kristina's suicide note, hoping Dr. K may have some insight to help us understand Kristina's mental and emotional condition. Only a few minutes in the waiting room, then we're ushered down a short hall into a small consulting room, nothing overdone or stuffy, comfortable and cozy, soft lighting, three chairs and a small desk. We greet each other carefully. Unfortunately, therapists have been targets for anger by family members after a suicide. Families want to know why therapies didn't help, or why

31

the patient was at risk. Kristina wasn't on medication and one of the questions I want answered is whether that made her suicidal.

"Our daughter often shared with us about her visits with you. She said you were helping her. She trusted you." I take a breath before going on. "We tried to be supportive ... but now ... it seems we didn't ask enough questions or understand enough about her condition. She never told us how dangerous anxiety could be. I let her down," I whisper.

"Kristina was in treatment for eighteen months," Dr. K begins. "Her diagnosis was anxiety with obsessive-compulsive tendencies, not active depression."

"Did she ever mention suicide or hating herself?" I probe.

"No, never. If she had, that would be another diagnosis entirely. I would have treated her differently."

She refers to her notes in the slender file on her desk. Dr. K is a thoughtful professional, gentle as she speaks with us. "I remember making a note in Kristina's file when our course of treatment ended. She was to call me in three to six months for a follow up visit. Also, I don't always write that a patient has been a delight to work with, but I did in her case. She was lovely. She seemed to be doing very well."

"We made a copy of her good-bye note for you. Would you read it and tell us what you think?" Bill gives Dr. K the copy. She reads then looks up at us, tears in her eyes.

"I'm so sorry. She was in such pain." After a few seconds she continues, "Kristina didn't talk about her achievements, especially not her sports or being an All-American. Her issues were fear in social situations, being in front of people, traveling, body image. And she always had a huge anxiety spike after being in the summer graduate school session. She was very anxious then. Very anxious. Anxiety is cumulative."

"We didn't know enough," I say. "Why was she discharged? Isn't anxiety a condition she'd have to manage all her life?"

"She ended a course of treatment and seemed to be doing well. She even told me she fell in love." A small smile accompanies this disclosure. "She wasn't confident about that yet. She said she'd fill me in when we met again for the follow up visit."

"Would medications have helped?"

"I'm not sure. Her work and health ethics were so strong we both agreed exercise, diet, and cognitive behavioral therapy were best for her."

"Well, thank you for seeing us," Bill stands and holds out his hand to shake hers.

I rise too, surprised there is so little information about our daughter, nothing even her therapist, a professional health care provider, could tell us to explain Kristina's sudden self-kill impulse. She presented no clinical symptoms that indicated she was or could become suicidal. It's a mystery that suicide really could have come out of the blue like that. I imagine it like a stalker, following her until she's weakest, when her reserves are low. Our daughter must have pondered suicide in secret, chosen not to say anything on purpose.

At the office door I turn and ask one more question, "Why did Kristina keep things from you, hide from the one person who really could have helped her?"

"People who have perfectionist tendencies want others to think highly of them. They cover up, wear a social mask. Failure is very public, not something they can handle. It doesn't fit their image of perfect. The more friends, the more people to see her weakness. That kind of thinking builds even more anxiety and depression can result. Kristina didn't make another appointment. I suspect she was deeply anxious; it always built when she was away at school where she especially wanted to succeed."

On the drive home, I recall a soccer game of Kristina's when we were alerted to her high pain threshold. She collided with another player on the field, breaking some of the wires from her braces. Normally parents are asked to stay back when their daughter is injured, but they called us over to the sidelines where Kristina held a cloth to her mouth.

Dr. Bierly was telling her, "I'm going to remove those wires from your cheek." He reached in, deftly removed the wires, and popped in an ice cube. "Suck on that ice cube for a minute. It will slow the bleeding and reduce swelling. It will hurt less too."

"It doesn't hurt," she mumbled.

John is a dentist, a good one. He had a concerned look when he turned to us and said, "She should see her orthodontist."

"No!" she protested. "I've got to get back in there. They're counting on me."

"If you get hit again, Kristina, it will hurt, possibly break off some more pieces," John cautioned.

She whipped out the ice cube. "I can do it. Just let me go back."

John motioned her to open up again. The bleeding had stopped and even though that side of her face looked puffy, she actually didn't look too bad.

"Okay. Keep away from any sharp elbows, and if you feel nauseous or start bleeding again, you've got to come back out. Agree?"

"Yes. Thanks."

Kristina walked over to her coach; he watched for the next opportunity to sub and then sent her back. John turned to us after seeing her race into position.

"I've seen her in practice. She has a high pain threshold. You've got to watch that."

"Watch it how?" I asked.

"Other injuries she's come back from would have stopped most players. If it's Kristina, she never gripes or complains. She plays the whole game. We can't take advantage of that strength. I worry that she won't know when to stop herself."

Sports culture encourages athletes to train and condition to incredible levels, sacrifice for the team, play through injuries, and suck up the pain. The thought of her playing until she collapsed, not knowing where her limits were or when to stop, seems like a sinister warning in hindsight. No, she didn't know how to stop herself.

12

The silence settles in on day five. No phone messages from Kristina. No gravel crunching in the drive as she parks her car and makes a quick stop at our house. No footsteps on stairs to her bedroom or exercise equipment in the basement.

After the calling hours, memorial service, and burial, our family and friends leave us to this unnatural quiet. I even miss hearing the wind chimes from Kristina's condo, packed away in my sister's suitcase for the flight to California yesterday. Unused to stillness, I decide to drive over, feed the cat, and just sit for a while.

I've been going over the puzzle in my head. So many questions. How long did our daughter suffer? What pain did she hide? How deep? How could I have been unaware of the despair and effort it took her to cover up? Why didn't any of us sense something had changed and gotten worse?

We know from her final note she yearned for a safe place. But I can only guess about what felt unsafe to her about the life she left. From her therapist's briefing it sounds like emotional and social safety were high on the list. I'm only just beginning to suspect how important her mask was, how she hid behind it to feel secure, and how critical it was to never let it slip, even if it might help her. Athlete, teacher, coach, girlfriend; all roles masked the real Kristina.

Once at her condo, I decide to make myself useful, maybe clean out her refrigerator, pick up the mail that hasn't been redirected to our address yet, water plants, and feed Annabelle. Instead of starting in the kitchen, I walk upstairs and look again at the evidence of her choice. Without consciously thinking about it I start picking up, toss the pill bottles, empty half-drunk water bottles, and untie the striped bed sheet from the leg of her bed to put it into the laundry basket in the bedroom. Then I change my mind and dump all the dirty clothes from the basket onto the floor; underwear, summer pajamas, workout shorts and tops. I scoop everything up and go into the bathroom where the washer and dryer are, grab used towels from the rack, stuff the washer tub, start the cycle, toss in some Tide powder, close the lid, and listen to the water fill up.

As the wash starts, I step back and burst into tears. Here I am in angry denial, cleaning innocent, everyday clothes I've seen Kristina wear hundreds of times, mixing them in with *those sheets* as if I'm removing whatever deadly suicidal impulse still lingers. It seems absolutely necessary to wash and dry her clothes, fold and return them to their normal places in her home. One other thing is also clear for me: I cannot throw anything out, not yet, not even the sheets that made a noose. So, I fold slowly, a lingering, careful, smoothing, tender folding. Deliberate. Even the offensive sheets are put back into the linen closet gently.

When I open drawers to put other things away I wonder why I'm bothering. I feel conflicted. Cleaning up the evidence feels good. Washing her clothes feels purposeful. But the thought of changing anything else makes me feel anxious. I simply don't have much left in me this day.

I walk out after doing laundry and later have to come back because I forgot to feed the cat.

13

"Mom, listen to this." Kristina is twenty in this memory and reading out loud to me from her summer reading book.

We are vacationing in Florida, visiting Bill's parents and relaxing on our favorite section of the Naples beach on the Gulf side. I am slathered in sunscreen and hiding under an umbrella. Kristina is half in, half out of the shade, book in, legs out. Excited and animated, she reads a section from *To the Lighthouse* by Virginia Woolf. Kristina loves reading, always has. Passionate about her books, she spends hours selecting them, looking at the print style, stroking the pages, feeling the paper stock, examining multiple copies bound different ways, savoring the smell and promise of each book she touches. A book is a sensual experience for Kristina, not just literary or intellectual. The form and function of a book interest her almost as much as its contents.

Kristina tells me she doesn't much care for critics or reading reviews; she likes expository writing and explications. When she reads she simply gets it, all the characters, plots, subplots, story lines, methods of construction, motifs, themes, and grammar. She engages herself in the process, surrendering completely to the journey of reading, digesting and ultimately understanding the work and as much of the writer as possible. Her commitment to studying literature is inspiring. I enjoy how she takes us all on the expeditions with her.

This same beach day she and Bill are talking about her college major and plans for after graduation.

"If somebody asks you what I want to do with my life, do you think you'd be able to tell them?" She let that sink in ... then adds, "Do you know that my dream is to be a writer?"

"Well ..." I heard Bill start.

But she interrupts him, "Do you know that by the time I'm forty I want to be able to call myself a novelist? Do you know that?"

In defense of her father and the wonderful relationship she shares with him, it is obvious she is being difficult on purpose with him that day. He remembers the conversation with a smile years later, just as she intends after this sensitive moment with him. Kristina knows Bill majored in English in college, went on to get his MBA, and made a career in financial investments.

"How could you leave the world of books, plays, writing?" she asks with total bewilderment. Bill tries to explain, saying things like you never lose anything you learn, even Chaucer has relevance today, and how he uses his writing skills in business every time he writes a report or sends an email message ... but she isn't buying it. I am being ignored completely and continue to keep mum while they are having this discussion.

"Daaad, that isn't writing! There is an incredible pleasure writing stories," Kristina told him. "When I read a story I truly enjoy, my heartbeat picks up, my thoughts move quickly and I become completely involved. I become part of their lives."

"That's a good thing, bud," he says.

"So, this feeling is what I wish for someone when they read my stories and poems," she wraps up.

As she and I sit on the beach later, I think about her habits. Like many writers, Kristina creates an environment and setting for her reading and writing. Pens, paper, type face she chooses for the font, styles of presentation, page format, and the position of the words on each page are objects of scrutiny and decision.

"Feel this!" she says, delighting in a paper she touches in the Papyrus store in the mall. "This paper is smooth and strong, protected with a chemical to keep it from yellowing in sunlight. Can you imagine, Mom, years from now, someone reaching for a book printed on this paper, knowing it is years and years old?"

I ooh and aah, appropriately I hope. My feelings for paper tend toward the best-weight-for-the-printer category, not much more. Yet I recall my own wonder as a history student when I would gaze on documents preserved for centuries, knowing the materials in the paper or skin, plus the chemical composition of the ink, made all the difference in conservation. I simply look at this a bit differently than Kristina; she breathes in both the paper and words.

In a book store or library I see her long fingers, graceful and gentle, handle books with an attitude of reverence. Only paperbacks she buys for study are marked and annotated. Marginalia, definitions, questions that arise while she reads, exclamations, observations, and tie-ins to other parts fill the pages of any book she is currently interacting with. It is a kinesthetic thing, her learning style too, as if moving words around, touching and writing are the only ways she can take the writer into herself.

Kristina never just reads a book, she engages with it completely in total immersion and she alternates reading with verbal comments aloud as if she has an audience. She loves hearing words read aloud, "Listen to this, Dad or Mom…" and off she goes reading. Every vacation Kristina packs books, lugging pounds in her backpack onto ferries, planes, buses, trains and cars without complaint, the only problem being where to find space for such a heavy carry-on.

"Honey, what have you got in here?" her Dad asks, teasing and affectionate. "Stones? Weights for working out? A friend you're hiding?"

"My books!" she grins and giggles.

Even shopping for vacation doesn't mean clothes to Kristina. Necessary, yes, but essential like her books, never. Books for her are life-giving, like breathing air.

Once, on a Cape Cod beach when she is six, I watch her. She's leaning back in a low beach chair, toes tucked into the sand. A white strip of zinc oxide coats her nose and her hair is pulled back in a ponytail. She's absentmindedly wiggling a loose tooth, all the while reading intently. She calmly pulls it out and lays it on a nearby tissue to save for the Tooth Fairy, never skipping a beat or losing her place on the page. The casualness of her gesture makes me grin, then giggle, then laugh so long and hard I am tearing. Oh, my precious reader and writer.

14

Counseling sessions with our minister, Gary Miller, start the first week after Kristina's death. Both nervous, Bill and I don't know what to expect. Less than one week and I am in so much physical and emotional pain I haven't gone back to work and can barely move. Everything just hurts. I've gone from shock and horror, appearing very organized in public, and now I'm shaky, raw and exposed. Even sunlight is painful on my skin when I sit outside. And besides, how dare the sun continue to rise and shine when our only child is dead? I feel the world should stop for something that important.

When we open the door and see Gary, Bill and I both start crying though we haven't said a word yet. "Hello, my dear friends," Gary hugs Bill with that kind of one arm guy-grip and handshake. A former football player, Gary has size and muscle, but is incredibly gentle and I'm certain he senses how close we are to breaking in two when he greets us.

Gary simply loves being a pastor, loves the people he serves. He walks people through life, celebrates with them in weddings and baptisms, honors them in concerts and memorial services. Early in his career Gary's love of music and jazz became a ministry of music, touring in the Celebration Road Show. We've heard him play his silver trumpet, worshiping with every note. We are grateful he immediately left church on that September 11 to hold our family together through tragedy and brokenness; starting then and continuing to guide us as we pick up the pieces, never the same again, trying to become whole.

This first visit the afternoon is gorgeous, cheerily affirmative in spite of our misery. We get settled in our living room at home in Farmington. Our pastor always has a shirt and tie on, sometimes a suit, other times a sports jacket, always a tie. He has strawberry blonde hair framing a kind face, one that breaks often into wide grins; humorous smiles reach his eyes. Even when thoughtful and sad, Gary's features are pleasant and welcoming. We see compassion in his visage.

Gary looks at us steadily and then begins. "One thing that will be very important to know is people grieve differently. And that's okay. There is no right or wrong way to grieve. You'll have feelings you've never had before. Memories of more than Kristina will surface – all these things are normal and we need to talk about them."

"I've been rereading Rabbi Kushner's book, *When Bad Things Happen to Good People*. He wrote his book after his son died," I offer.

After a few moments Gary leans over, "Go on."

"I don't feel angry at God. I don't feel anger toward Kristina. I just feel so sad that she made a decision to leave us." I stop, think about what to say next. "To me, Kristina's dying was not God's plan. God didn't jump in to save her. That just doesn't happen. God didn't plan Kristina's death to teach me a lesson either."

"I agree. God weeps with us now," Gary says.

I hurry to say, "I mean, I know there is a lesson in this tragedy, a lesson for all of us, but that is not the purpose. God didn't take her away; we didn't drive her away. Because of her disease she chose a way out from pain. That's different from rejecting us and love."

"What do you think the purpose of her dying is?"

"There is no purpose. I think Kristina suffered so deeply she didn't see any other solution. She loved us, even worried about leaving us behind, wrote it in her note. Yet love wasn't enough."

I am squeezing my crossed arms. There's a little silence, each of us thinking and hurting. There's a great deal bottled up inside so I continue. "In my heart I know God didn't make this happen. She did. Her disease did. The school did. We all did." I hear myself and it sounds like whining and blaming when there's really no blame.

Gary looks at me, then Bill, compelling us to listen closely.

"Remember what I said in Kristina's service?" Bill and I nod. "It's not God's will that even one of His children should suffer. Kristina did the best she could with all that she had to give. It was enough for everyone except Kristina. Her well ran dry."

We nod again. The image was very powerful at the time and still is. The thought of Kristina giving, giving and all of us taking, taking is sorrowful beyond belief. We drained her.

"Kristina was someone who gave until she had nothing left to give," Gary pauses. Bill reaches for a tissue, hands me one too. Our eyes are streaming. We suffer hearing Gary's words. "For whatever reason, Kristina did not see her impact on others and what you saw in her. And eventually the well was empty."

"That's why we hurt so much now. She didn't believe in herself. She always said we're her parents and supposed to say good things about her. Why didn't she believe us or others who praised her?" I ask.

"Her disease and mental health condition got worse, got away from her. That 'dis-ease' means she was not at ease with herself, profoundly, deeply and fatally."

"I looked up the origin of the word suicide ... one Latin source is *sui cado*, to let one's self fall. She fell too," I say. My imagined vision of her climbing the balcony and moving off into air to hang herself comes back.

"When I was in the car today," Bill says, "I was listening to the radio and heard a Journey song she used to play all the time when she was in middle school. For a minute she was back here with me. I look for signs now."

"They're there," Gary agrees.

Bill continues. "My friend Butch told me I'll dream of her, see her walking down the street. She'll appear all the time. Don't be afraid. Don't think I'm going crazy."

Gary nods with agreement. "You and Kristina will find a way for your spirits to keep connected."

And so our counseling starts, each hour begins mostly as conversation about where we are in our pain and memories of Kristina, how hard the grief work is, how hard life is now, and then on to the spiritual questions. We need these faith journey discussions with our minister. We don't know where this tragedy will take us; what we know is we want to stay married and heal together. Each week Bill and I feel the pressure and emotions build up. We are needy, anxious for our next counseling hour together. Gary encourages us to talk, talk, talk - through the pain, through the feelings, through life reconstruction, through the tough choices.

There are years ahead of us to survive Kristina's suicide. Already we divide life into before and after her death. We listen to others deeply, aren't shy about alerting parents to support their children's mental health. Gary tells us church members are calling each week or dropping into his office to ask, "What can we do to help the Stahls?" Many feel clueless; they haven't experienced something like this. Some feel fear, worried suicide could happen to their children too.

"They've been writing, telephoning, bringing food – our church friends have been wonderful," Bill says. "We've had incredible conversations with people about their own losses too, things they never told us before."

I think about how hard it is to attend Sunday services, mostly because we cry so much these days. The messages touch us differently now. The music is emotional. People look at us, worried about our pain.

"Let them love you. Feel the strength of their love," Gary says. "Want to write something for the newsletter?" That idea scares me. I can barely think and walk at the same time. Gary continues, "They want to know you're going to be all right." *Well, they'll just have to wait.*

15

The September 30, 2002 edition of the school newspaper, *KO News*, is delivered to our house by one of Kristina's friends. "We thought you and Mr. Stahl would like a copy," she tells me.

The front page headline reads **KO mourns loss of beloved teacher** and there is a photo of Kristina taken her first year teaching, along with the caption, *Ms. Kristina Stahl '95, English teacher and coach, died tragically September 11, 2002. Students and faculty grieve for the community's loss.*

The article has an excellent recap of her school career, quotes from the Head of School and colleagues, and a description of measures taken to support students and faculty in the days following her death with assemblies, home room discussions, and counseling. There are interviews with key people about how the school is coping and coming together for good.

Inside the edition there are reflections written by several students, beautiful moving tributes and fond remembrances of Kristina as their teacher, coach, friend, and role model. One student refers to Kristina as the "quote goddess" and remembers one in particular posted on her office wall:

> *For yesterday I hold no apologies.*
> *For tomorrow I offer no answers.*
> *Today is a gift: I will honor it by fully living in it.*

They don't credit who wrote it and I'd really like to know why she chose it. There's so much I don't know about our own daughter.

16

Mindless, everyday tasks, feel impossibly empty without Kristina in our lives. Cleaning litter boxes, doing laundry, raking leaves, and endless chores fill the spaces from her absence.

Like any parent, anxious imaginings came occasionally when Kristina was growing up, mostly when she was a teenager. Travel, drugs, alcohol, date rape, traffic accidents ... the stuff of nightmares that visit parents even when we know everything possible is being done to ensure their safety. Our letting go meant adventure for her, and it was necessary to grow.

Years after Kristina took a school trip to England, I discover a story she'd written about a night in London at the Hippodrome, a huge entertainment venue. She never liked crowds and her anxiety level would soar in those days, causing panic attacks. One night Kristina bolted, desperate to get out of the club with too many people, too close. After taking the London tube and making her way back to the hotel, she realized she hadn't told her teachers she was leaving, only her friends. The school wouldn't have let students go out at night alone, so she worried about being sent home. There were several calls to us to find the best outcome. She did stay. That whole experience must have sparked a story idea.

In her story there are graphic descriptions of groping hands, sweaty bodies, threatening music, tears, and descriptions of young people edging the dance floor. The crowd scares the main character who sees drugs passed and lots of drinking. She thinks of it as a "pervasive atmosphere of threat." The girl sees no easy escape from a maze of loud dark rooms filled with strangers. She experiences a chase through the city's underground system. She fears attack.

The story reads like a terrifying horror movie, nightmarish, nothing we imagined or Kristina ever discussed after her trip. Years later my heart races as I read; her terror bursts from every page. It doesn't feel like fiction.

17

At the end of September, nearly three weeks after Kristina's suicide, her boyfriend Chris parks his green pick-up truck in the drive. It's loaded with packing boxes from her school office.

Last week Chris told me he's keeping busy; he's back in school teaching on a half-day schedule, hoping to provide a sense of continuity and support for students who are missing Kristina and worrying about him too. I'm sure his presence helps, and I can only imagine how hard it is to pack up her office, touch things that are familiar and special for him as well.

He's looking thinner this week than the last time I saw him at the Porter's game. There are taut lines in his face and he appears tired. The autumn warmth is still with us, though not as hot as it's been. In the dusk now there are a few fireflies that flit about as Chris steps out of the truck onto the gravel driveway.

Just a few days earlier Bill and I visited the school campus. We have a sad good-bye of our own. The Head of School, Dr. Lee Levison, greets us. He's a tall man with a quiet presence and kindly demeanor, a former athlete. His remarks during Kristina's memorial service about her "heavy lifting" work ethic and being a scholar athlete were inspiring and gave comfort to the mourners by offering his perspective on Kristina's professional life as a dedicated teacher and coach.

From 1993 to 2000 I served on the school's Board of Trustees and very much enjoyed being part of the educational community in a practical way. When Kristina became a member of the faculty I felt even more committed. Now, Bill and I are talking with the school about a lasting contribution in Kristina's name. Our idea is set up a faculty development program, one that will mentor new teachers, acknowledge and address their educational needs, the insecurity, stress and anxiety teaching brings. We hope the donations that have been arriving every day since her death will cover startup costs to begin an endowment for the future.

"First, I want to show you the tribute wall set up for students and faculty. It's in the Roberts building," Lee says.

We walk along the paved path to the large auditorium building next door, enter the glass doors, and cross a polished floor to the gallery located near the auditorium doors. The location is both private and accessible, a quiet area for students to come, to remember. The walls and standing pedestals are brightly lit. There is an abundance of postings on the gallery wall. Everywhere we look there are posters, messages, photos, flowers, and student writings.

One pedestal holds a vase of cut flowers, another, the Girls Varsity Soccer team scrapbook of photos and player descriptions. Next to it is a stack of small papers, pens, and push pins. Visitors are encouraged to write a few words on the paper, say their goodbyes. One message, posted on the board with hundreds of fluttering pieces of paper, catches my eye:

Ms. Stahl, How could you? I am so angry you left us.

Bill and I read notes out loud to each other as we move around the space. Most praise her teaching and how she helped them. Several are bewildered, confused. The majority are sad about her death and the fact she won't be in their lives any longer.

Our next stop is her office. She had arranged an attractive place for students and players. There's a cane basket chair near her desk and posters of runners and athletes. Kristina typed up quotes from her favorite writers and posted them on every available inch of wall space. I recognize a small Easter basket I'd hidden for her one year with three marble eggs inside labeled Dream, Wonder, and Hope. Taped behind her chair is the poem What Is Success? by Ralph Waldo Emerson. Without knowing it is one of her favorites, we had included it as a reading in her memorial service.

Bill points out photos he likes on the bookshelves, walls, file cabinets, and bulletin board. In them, Kristina is always smiling, arms hugging others, together with her students, teams, teachers and friends. In the corner there are three teddy bears dressed in sports outfits, gifts from players. I pick one up to hold as I walk around the room. On one shelf there are at least ten coffee mugs lined up near a hand-me-down coffee pot from us. I remember what she told me just after school started. "I'm going to have to fix only decaf at school this year. That's all I drink now. Hope the students are okay with that."

Now Chris is at our house bringing home her things. I walk out the front door to help unload. "Hey, Chris. Thanks for packing up. We're grateful."

"You're welcome. I had helpers," he says.

For the next few minutes we make the sad trek from the truck, into the house, through the hall, up the stairs and into the bedroom Kristina lived in until three years ago when she rented her own apartment. Back and forth, back and forth, we lift boxes out of the truck, climb stairs, and stack them in her room. I've put up some additional bookshelves to hold everything from school, condo, and home. For now, however, Chris and I don't unpack, we simply put everything on the floor.

"Do you still want to look through her writing? Not too tired?" I ask.

He nods first *yes* then shakes *no*, reminding me of how often Kristina used to tell me that I had a habit of stringing together two questions. She suggested I think like a teacher, one question at a time, no more.

We head downstairs to my basement office. What a contrast mine is to hers. It's spare with only a few photos on the walls and a computer on the desk. There is a workout area around the corner. The original idea was for me to work, then take breaks to exercise. At least that was the plan.

Now I look at the treadmill and remember seeing Kristina there. She often came to jog and keep me company while I worked. She positioned a full length mirror in front of her to correct her stance and stride. However, when she wasn't there the mirror blocked the TV and stash of DVDs, my normal approach to exercising, so I always put it away when I jogged.

Kristina would buzz in with a cheery smile, saying, "Hi Mom," then take out the mirror, punch in her settings, and get down to business. She dressed in blue jogging shorts and top. She wore a headset and paced to the music, occasionally glancing over at me to grin and give me a thumbs-up. She also kept a log of her workouts. One time I saw it open and read the latest entry: 47 minutes jog, 15 minutes free weights, 576 calories burned. I was hugely impressed. A good day for me barely earns a snack in total calories.

Kristina was training for a half marathon scheduled in Boston the next month. It registers I need to check with her friend, Allison, and see if there are hotel reservations to cancel or other arrangements to change, a thought that shifts me back abruptly. It seems all I'm doing is rewinding and unwinding her life.

My desk where Chris is seated is positioned directly in front of the double doors for the best view of the woods near our house. Interesting. I always sit to look outside. Kristina had her office desk face inside the room, the windows behind her, so she would greet students as they come in.

Right now there are piles everywhere along with a carton of her writing journals, her laptop, and boxes of discs neatly labeled in her clear print. It was important for me to bring back her writing from the condo. I scoured shelves, cabinets and closets to find the journals, tucked away in a corner bookcase in her living room, partially hidden behind wrapping paper and gift bags. Upstairs in her study I located college and graduate school notebooks and correspondence. In her bedroom I found the most recent journal she'd been writing in, one with a smooth black leather cover.

I need to figure it out, am compelled to find out everything I missed. Her writing, I believe, is the critical first step. Somewhere in there I'd find it I'm sure. Although I didn't put it into words, deep down I knew there is something we would find.

Chris is powering up her laptop; the background screen saver is a Georgia O'Keeffe painting. How she loved that artist, decorating her bedroom with prints and asking for coffee table art books at Christmas.

"I don't know her password," Chris says.

"Try 'kristina' in lower case," I suggest. That works. Chris logs on and begins to scan files on the hard drive.

"There isn't much here," he says.

Recently, her old laptop crashed so she lost all her stored work, mostly school documents. After that debacle and a new laptop, she started using the school server for academics and coaching, then backed up her personal writing on external disks in case of another meltdown.

"I'll start with the disks here and check the school files later."

"What about email?" I ask. She's had an AOL account.

"Schieby said the last she received was September 9. Kristina wrote her about a student giving her a hard time. Ron, her department supervisor, talked with her about it."

Schieby has forwarded that one to me also. Kristina sounded stressed but seemed to be handling it. The email is remarkably upbeat. Most of the message is about how Kristina planned to help the student.

"Did she tell you about this taunting student too?" I ask Chris.

"Yes. She had soccer practice then dropped by my office. We talked a bit about him. Then she gave me a hug and went out for her run." He pauses then continues, "It really bothered her. She was anxious about being able to turn this guy around." That afternoon was the last time Chris saw Kristina.

I turn back to her box of writing. It was her habit to start poems and short stories in draft version, not finished by any means, mixing those in with personal entries. The box holds so much – twenty three journals. I feel lightheaded and nervous, worried about violating her privacy, yet I have to know, so I start with the one I picked up from her nightstand and read a November 2001 entry:

I am scared. This morning – felt that feeling, death was inevitable or is it inevitable, and is it getting closer? I keep thinking of it. Keep thinking of it. Death would be so much easier – but what is this trouble? I am so ashamed – I have no trouble. There is nothing wrong, nothing is wrong, so many things are right. Why can't I count the right things?

Her handwriting looks jagged, not her normal handwriting. The discovery bubbles up, blooms, inches through, and bursts with an emotional force until I'm panting. My hands shake so badly I put the journal down. Something is going to terrify me even more. I know I'm close to it.

Next I feel anger, a raw, mother outrage. Here we are, in my basement office, two people who loved Kristina deeply, questioning all that we thought to be true and real about her. I don't have a clue why this has happened to her or to us either. All I know is her suicide is bringing me doubt, changing my view of the past and future forever.

I hear a noise coming from across the room. While I was reading and immersed in my own pain, I had forgotten Chris.

"I think I found something." His voice is grave. He speaks carefully. "When she had a panic attack I thought she wanted me to leave." Chris fills me in. "We were at her condo, talking about the future, maybe leaving for other positions. We were in the living room and she was getting anxious. Then she started crying. When I reached out to hug her, she raised her hand to stop me, waved me away. I thought she meant for me to go. She typed this up afterward when she was at school doing lesson plans." He reads the entry:

It is almost 9:00 am and I am tired. I slept fitfully, without rest. I am anxious. I am ashamed of my behavior, of my lack of control and foresight. I am scared. I wish for time to pass quickly. I wish for strength.

I hear his confidence and I feel weakened, jealous of his ability to stand. I recognize our positions. I see my fear and anxiety opposed to his strength. I have exposed myself in a way that must be unattractive. I worry that he will stop loving me. I am focused on this, however destructive.

Her words confirm her anxiety condition was stronger than ever. This panic attack was triggered by talking about their future. I wonder how often she was she having panic attacks. Several times a day? At night alone? I am wild with anger. I have lots of targets – school, doctors, friends, and especially me – all of us who hadn't seen the pain or helped her get back into treatment. I look over and see Chris' own stricken look.

Shaking, wanting to lash out at a world not safe enough for her, I hold all that roiling, dark anger inside. I don't know what else to do about these extreme feelings. We now know she was suffering from anxiety deep enough to send Chris away rather than have him witness a panic attack.

I draw a deep breath and read out loud to Chris from the journal I've been holding:

Something has shifted. I cannot communicate. I am afraid to ask or share or express myself. This writing is making it worse. I cannot cry again. I cannot show such weakness. This is exhausting. I am afraid. This huge condo and I am scared. I don't know what to do. I don't know how to see what I am feeling. I sense such horrible doom, such –

I shut the cover, overwhelmed for now. This brief look into her writing is wrenching. Going through all the rest is going to take a great deal of time and energy.

Chris leaves, both of us shaken and saddened.

18

My immediate plan is to gather back every note, letter, card, and stray piece of paper Kristina has written on. Eventually I'll read through it all and type up her journal entries by date, sort through to find clues. It will be like reconstructing her life or profiling for a case, especially the pieces we missed. I feel intense urgency. I need to be convinced that her death wasn't an accident or call for help that went too far.

I'm alone in Kristina's former bedroom here at home with the carton of journals. Maybe I should simply toss them? I have such doubts. Kristina's diaries have always been private, the one place she went to be with herself and her own thoughts, respected, inviolate. I pull back my hand, wishing I could talk with her instead; ask if she really wanted to die. I mull over possibilities, wonder if the answer is in her writing or not, acknowledge I need to know one way or the other and eventually talk myself into reading.

Less hesitant now, I pull out one from her early years. Winnie the Pooh is on the cover, a gift from one of her middle school friends. Her handwriting is rounded, not like her adult style that was part print, part cursive, angled and artistic looking. The youthful script brings back memories of homework assignments and her first little notes to us. I leaf through the pages and find short stories and essays with titles such as *What Friendship Means to Me, Secret for Two,* and *My Favorite Animal.* There's a series of adventures about a mermaid who rides on a sea turtle's back.

Her handwriting changes several times. She switches to tiny precise printing when she writes about being angry or upset. In a section where she writes about a boy she's interested in the handwriting goes loopy with flourishes. After reading several more stories I flip to the back cover. There she's written *Kristina, do this and do this, do, do, do, do* – twenty times near the spine. By the last *do* the ink is grooved into the cardboard, pushed hard with frustration.

I upend the carton onto her bed and spread out all the journals. What an array. Some are simple spiral-bound lined notebooks, several are beautiful, covered in leather and soft to the touch. Many are hard-bound and quite a few have decorative covers. There's a beautiful Asian style journal that runs from September 1 to November 9, 2000. Inside she's settled into what I recognize as her current distinctive handwrit-ing style and the color of the ink changes frequently – black, blue, terra cotta, teal and dark brown. She's inserted typed love poems. There are two sunflower journals, one from her teens and one from college years.

Over the next two weeks I read everything she wrote from when she was eight until twenty-five years old, and her last week of life. Some-times I find myself smiling, hear her voice in my head as she labors through friendships, slights, misunderstandings, break ups, and the de-mands of teen years. There's a special journal for her trip to England with high school friends. Part scrapbook, part travel guide, she writes about her classes, sightseeing, and her reactions to everything. There are tickets and playbills inserted between pages, a few Tube receipts, photos, and some programs from touring museums, galleries and theaters.

I'm relieved at how normal most of this reads. She gets upset and rants on friends or people who snub her at school. She scolds herself for what she thinks is "stupid stuff." She complains about her clothes, hair, and weight. She even writes about not wanting to feed the cats or clean up the dishes after meals. I'm lulled into thinking everything is going to turn out fine, forgetting for surreal moments that it hasn't; this isn't a story with a happy ending.

A picture of Kristina emerges and I think about what I'm learning, whether or not it has anything to do with her suicide. The girl and young woman I see collects quotes and poems over many years, interspersing them throughout her reflections. She thinks about how words are used, is careful and purposeful with her writing. She survives adolescence, which is to say she has quarrels with best and former best friends all the time and there are misunderstandings she works out on paper. She pass-es notes in class those pre-texting days, and she saves responses, folded over and over to palm easily and not be detected, a thrill students with electronic technology now wouldn't appreciate.

Kristina draws cartoons and doodles. One page shows a young girl in twenty different outfits and hair styles, dressed for sports, occupations, travel, casual, dressy, special events, costumes. Intricate flower designs illustrate paper edges. I see broad flat strokes, rounded curly letters, deliberate sharp printing, erratic phrases with many dashes and unfinished thoughts that thrust out, jagged messy words filled with pain, fluid cursive for pages of lovely lyrical thinking, and energetic half and half writing that is crisp, pointy and very precise with a super-fine pen. Off and on there's calligraphy. The variety is revealing. I get a sense of her feelings before even reading one word. I figure out she prefers unlined paper; journals with lines are regularly abandoned halfway through. Sometimes she stops a journal abruptly, some she stops then returns to months or years later. Most endings coincide with a calendar year, an event, a trip, or a break up.

Although we had talked about her romances, I now read what she loves about men and women, expressing her love in beautiful letters and poems. She writes of the giddy, fascinated, infatuated, and enamored stages, along with her actions, what she's wearing, and their conversations. She is desperately unhappy when her lovers leave her, which always seems to happen. She writes many letters urging them to come back and love again. Some of her best poems are about the loss of love.

And when you leave

Who are you to me I want to know
Your face is something
I see me in
Some laugh I've heard before
Some touch I knew it once
Though it wasn't here before
Where have you come from and why now
When I didn't need to find you
You came for yourself
Or did you come at all
How'd you get here
And where's it going
Your skin smells like home
Your hands at my neck
And in my hair
Pulling me back from where I've been
Your eyes I can't let go
And your face
It's captured in my own
I wonder what I've done

And what it means
Or is it nothing –
Tell me this is it something
I thought I didn't need to know
Where'd you come from
And where are you going
If you leave me let me know
I thought I knew what I was doing
I guess I do
But what is this –
Some weird thing I know it's good
What will I learn about me
And learn to give you
Back again if you stay
And when you leave
Will I be a better me
And will I miss you now that I know you
Or do I know you at all
Where's it going and why do I care
You've caught me here and
I laugh because I am happy
June 3, 2000

In some of the writing she criticizes herself about what she shouldn't have done and what would have been better. She blames herself for feeling too needy, too clingy, too weak, too emotional – too everything – laying fault on herself. In college and afterward, not once does she get angry with the loves who leave her, a big difference from her teenage years. I prefer her honest anger to self-recrimination. Finally, I read how she and Chris find each other and love, but her entries sound uncertain:

Lucky coincidence that now, at this time, Chris and I meet in such a wonderful place. Does he think me too young, too immature, too naïve? Does he think me inexperienced – lousy – volatile? Am I too explosive? What does he need that I cannot give him? Will I succeed? I don't fear these things. I raise them as questions to recognize possible anxieties.

She sketches a picture of how she sees the future, having doubts about her writing too. One section moves me deeply:

How am I so unsatisfied with my writing, when really I live to have complete faith in the idea that I am going to be a writer, a

55

publisher, a producer of words.

I wonder what will become of everything that I have started to write about in this computer, or all of the worthless and scribbled stories I have copied into my numerous journals.

Kristina writes that she's afraid of her moods, knows how they grab and hold onto her. She becomes repetitive, tackling the same thought from all different directions, a sign of obsessing, unable to let go of a thought until she's worn it down. Occasionally, I feel her spinning out of control; she writes to rein herself back in:

Tremor ... my heart hurts so much. I am so afraid of life. I am so afraid of life. I just whispered, "Get your shit together." I think it practically worked. Why am I so serious? Why do so many feelings haunt me? Do I even know what I'm saying? Say it again and aim for its meaning.

"Wake up" – to what though? This isn't a nightmare – this is real. And what do I do with this mess now?

Often she writes positive affirmations, tells herself to believe, to be strong. When good friends give her advice she writes that down, sounding grateful for their insight. She also writes down dreams she's had, many very pleasant. A few times she describes her nightmares and analyzes them, often linking them to a problem she's coping with or a worry that won't go away.

The first two years of college she complains about drinking too much and feeling uncomfortable being out of control, eventually writing about how disgusted she is with herself and how she'll change. By her junior and senior years she recognizes when her thoughts are scary under the influence of alcohol, scolds herself and gets control, wanting to be a better role model for younger teammates especially.

There are typed pages inserted between entries. She's lyric and detailed in her descriptions, especially about the people who become friends, coaches, and faculty. Her maturing writing style is powerful. She finished stories and poems, working through drafts and edits, multiple cross outs. I have a very clear sense of Kristina emerging as a writer from these pages.

For most of her journals, Kristina is a young girl growing up with the usual school, friend and family events. A few tender references to

Bill and me as parents warm me. Then I read many complaints about us, things I agree with as I follow along. No teen would want to join parents watching Dick Clark on New Year's Eve! I'm not surprised entries about us become infrequent, especially after she goes to college. We don't figure prominently in her life; we're background players and supporting cast.

I also notice some gaps, times and events Kristina didn't write about. One area is when my parents, her grandparents, both died suddenly within six months of each other. She loved them and I know she grieved for them when alone and away at college. However, there is a beautiful poem written for Grandpa Arentzen at Christmas 1995 as a present, a long poem of admiration and encouragement about his suffering after a stroke. It starts with this line: Your eyes give such light to a darkness you battle within.

Kristina is thrilled and challenged as a teacher and coach. Many entries about teaching. She praises several, some of them her former teachers, and she writes down their advice. Her descriptions of former coaches and wanting to pass on a legacy are touching. Typically she blames herself when students and athletes don't do well in class or in sports. She feels responsible, not just accountable. There are more clues to her state of mind:

All of this fear and self-doubt keeps creeping. Even here. These moments of cluelessness or isolation – I am isolated. I am alone.

Concerned that I've chosen the wrong role for myself. What makes a good coach? What makes a good teacher?

Some of the most revealing entries are about her panic attacks. I find one written after I telephoned her when she was feeling ill. She was newly living in an apartment above an office in West Hartford then, working hard, often getting sick. I offered to come over with dinner. Now I feel awful to learn I had been a trigger for her anxiety and didn't even know it:

The day is grey outside. I feel weighted down with the sickness held in my chest. Mom just called. Her concern ignited an attack. I can't wail up here so it hurt to cry quietly. Distorting my face without sound. No one to see or hear me. Terrible anxiety, self-induced.

Stop this. Get out of here. But I wanted to work. So much work to do tomorrow. Don't think so much, please. Relax. Breathe. Don't let the absence and gaps push you out. I feel as though I am reverting. Terrible laughter below. Damn. Such contrasting emotions.

Pretend for a moment that you do have control and that your fear and anxiety are those things that convince you otherwise. Do not pray for the release, for the imagined life beyond, just to stop this fabricated suffering.

Sometimes she writes in the third person as "she" or "her," a form of separating her inner, frightened self from her outer, social self. Other images are scattered in the recent entries:

At least Death has left me alone today – strange that I just wrote that as if Death was a person...what is this mess?

She has an entry that touches on Virginia Woolf and suicide:

Water imagery seeps into my language – Woolf's influence. Can't believe that she drowned herself. Creative people can be troubled. They see things differently – is that me? Am I creative? Where do I fall? Is that a silly cliché? Where do I fall? Anywhere but here. Nowhere.

The last years of her entries are almost unbearable for me to read; how awful it was for her to live through anxiety, panic attacks and strong emotions that feel out of control. I find words and thoughts that are suicidal, although she doesn't use the word suicide. The code for her suicide ideation is "the option." This entry is the strongest clue to her mental state. She was seeing her own death as a way out, a choice she was considering making if the pain got too great:

Why must I feel anxiety as I see time spread out in front of me on a calendar? Why do I suffer from fear and worry? Why am I so afraid to fail? I am scared of myself. My eyes cross, my heart quivers – death, she is here in my chest – pounding – the option ... always the pathetic option. There is nothing to say. I could never give up but I so want to sometimes. There are no promises, wherever you go. Stop spiraling. You are doing this to yourself. Stop writing.

The final entries are few and far between. They dwindle and fade with many months in between. I feel great sadness and wish she'd shared these suicidal thoughts. She writes most with Chris in mind, but he didn't see her words or suspect. Her handwriting gets smaller and smaller, another clue that she's closing in on herself. She becomes more and more afraid of her thoughts.

As her illness and anxiety increase she writes less. When she stops going to her therapist she writes how she expects to be cured and able to handle her anxiety now like an adult. Nowhere does she write about having an ongoing condition that needs to be managed, but can't be cured.

By the time she contemplates *the option* she writes about herself as weak, subject to feelings and emotions she'd like to control, not control her. Her fear is very real, almost constant. Her voice is lost completely the last year, only one journal, very few entries. She's frightened of writing more.

Through all the last painful entries I'm caught up in her daily battle to convince herself she will be well and strong, that she has value, that her world is anxious only if she makes it so:

Trying to keep things simple, focus on positive thinking ... body image issues, confidence and self-consciousness issues, emotional and social issues ... had a long conversation w/Dr. K tonight. Always feel good, though sometimes mentally exhausted. So much time passed since our last April meeting ... I didn't like having to recall so much, though I did want to share...I never seem to keep things to myself.

She writes affirmations to be strong for teaching, mantras such as "this too shall pass." She fights for herself with determination and courage. With no warning, the handwritten journal entries end with a last entry that is especially heartbreaking:

I feel confused, insecure, doubtful. I am scared. I need to relax, to be patient. How have I lost focus? How have I lost my confidence? I fear this. I fear losing, through pushing to know and understand. I am ashamed. I am embarrassed. I don't want to move, to leave, to abandon Chris. I fear if I did, he would not follow me.

Now that I've finished I'm exhausted, completely broken open emotionally after absorbing her fight. My eyes are gritty and sore from reading for days and days. It's time for me to surrender, let the mystery go for now.

19

The last time Bill and I saw Kristina alive was September 8, 2002. We had a standing family date for dinner out Sunday nights if she was free. For a few years she rented an apartment next to a public parking lot, across from the post office and Bricco, a popular restaurant. The apartment was above a financial services office and, in one of those life coincidences, the assistant who worked there, Pat, had been employed at the insurance company and working with Kristina's grandfather. They were delighted to have her as their renter with a white kitten upstairs.

"Kristina?" Pat would call up the stairs. "Looking for Annabelle? She's down here with us again."

Sunday evenings we would drive in, park in the lot nearby, and walk to Bricco. Sometimes we ate outside on the patio to enjoy the breeze and people walking by on the sidewalk, sometimes we sat at the bar watching a game on TV, and sometimes we went into main dining room for more room to include her friends as guests. Bricco is our family place away from home.

That last Sunday dinner together, Kristina was finishing up work at school and met us there. She joined us at a booth inside, looking tired and drawn. When our meals arrived she listlessly picked at her prawn dish, drank little from her glass of white wine, and didn't seem to have any appetite.

"What's wrong?" I ask.

She shakes her head. "It's my classroom program for school. Most students are respectful and accountable for their work. Their parents signed off on the agreement. I just don't have a good feel about one student. He's new at the school."

"Have you talked with Ron?"

"Yes, then he told Ms. Hanson, the department head, and that was embarrassing. I feel like they want to be supportive, but ... " Her voice fades. I notice how thin she looks. Kristina has been slender since ending her national level sports competition, but not quite this size. She's lost weight.

"Are you eating, honey?"

"It's just a few pounds. I've been running lots of miles. Once I start eating at the school cafeteria it will come back fast enough." After dinner - most of which Kristina takes home in a doggy bag - we pause on the sidewalk outside.

"Anyone want an ice cream?" she asks.

"No, I ate more than you did, but I'll walk with you," I say. She looks disappointed.

"Really, I want to," I add more enthusiastically. "Dad will go ahead home. You can drop me off afterward."

"No, that's okay. Thank you for dinner. I love you guys."

She hugs us, then turns and walks away. Once across the street I had a gut feeling, a premonition that I wouldn't see her again. I shook it off as worried-mother behavior, but still turned for another glimpse of her walking toward her car. I didn't tell Bill about my strange feeling, just commented, "She looks so alone. I think I should have gone with her. She's working too hard." Kristina called us that evening to say thank you again for dinner. I asked if she went for her ice cream cone. "No," she said, she'd changed her mind.

In retrospect, perhaps if I'd walked with her she might have talked. I might have sensed how deeply depressed and hopeless she was feeling. She seemed tired from everything – school, her workouts, helping run soccer camp as well as coaching the Junior Varsity team alone, having no time for Chris, preparing for school to start, planning lessons – do, do, do. Did I feel she was at risk and in danger? No, only stressed out and needing a break.

When she called two days later, the night she killed herself, I still didn't see these things all converging and overwhelming her.

20

Never a friendly cat before Kristina's death, Annabelle becomes increasingly withdrawn. We haven't decided what to do with her yet. Since our own two cats are old and feeble the vet cautions us not to bring her into our home. Every day we go to the condo in the morning to feed Annabelle breakfast, then return in the afternoon for her dinner. I talk to her, sit on the couch to attract her for petting, and try to calm her. Her trauma is deep and she continues to droop more and more. When I get out the cat toys, try to play with her, Annabelle ignores me.

One evening I am upstairs in the condo, packing some things in the study, preparing for the move out. I keep looking at the balcony spot where Kristina embraced her hanging sheet. I need to work quickly, finish and leave.

I pack cleats and athletic gear to donate to soccer teams, then go downstairs. Annabelle is waiting for me, well not exactly me. I try to comfort her using soothing words and cautious motions. One green eye, one blue, look at me; she's lost that frantic wild look. Annabelle slowly turns her back on me and pads away to her nest under the hem of the curtains by the glass sliding doors in the living room.

No, I am not her person, her Kristina, I'm just the woman she tolerates to feed her and clean the litter box. Poor abandoned pet, witness to her person's horrifying struggle and death.

21

Grave tending. The first week after her burial, I go to the cemetery to weed, water, arrange, search for Kristina's spirit somehow. The term grave tending sounds old fashioned, from a bygone age when cemeteries were designed as parks too, areas for socializing after church and taking strolls with family members or visitors, weaving together the past and present. People planted gardens there, both flowers and some decorative vegetables.

Today I come with one of Kristina's favorite Sting albums, The Sea. Schieby had mentioned Kristina always played this particular CD in the dorm when she was happy. When I chose it to bring with me I was surprised at how extensive and broad-ranging her music collection was, noting several musicians she collected over many years. I flipped through the collection for at least an hour, taking in her interests, touching hard plastic discs as if they held a secret. I thought I might learn about who she really was, what she really liked, what she treasured above other sounds.

I turn the engine off and leave the car door open. The music ebbs and flows with steel bands and island melodies, Calypso themes, beautiful lyrics about people and sea dwellers. It's uplifting.

"I thought you would like to hear your favorite music again," I tell Kristina as I stand by the grave.

The new family stone is in place, lettered with three generations of Stahls – Raymond, Anna Louise, William, Karin and Kristina – birthdates accompany our names. Only one date of death. I felt uncertain when the funeral director first proposed this marker style. I don't know, maybe I thought she should have her own stone, something special, a quote maybe, carved just for her. Apparently cemetery guidelines influenced our choice, I don't recall the details, and I see everything is flat in this new section.

"The heat's over, honey. It's cool soccer weather. Just the way you like it," I murmur to her.

I tug crabgrass. I'm relentless, merciless, scattering loose dark soil with my near-violent pulls. I don't want to be doing this. I hate it. The pile grows. Soon I've practically denuded the new grass planted that was battling with the weeds for space. I stop, stand up, brush off my damp-dirt knees and pick up the pile.

Her grave is near the river. A steep bank leads down to the curving bed, shallow and muddy this fall day. I clutch the earthy refuse, planning to fling it over the sides. Instead, all I manage is a feeble release for only a few feet.

I gaze out over the water at a flock of Canada geese floating there, resting after migratory practice runs. They look beautiful and strong, elegant with their crisp banded necks and long shapely beaks. Kristina loved watching them in the sky and feeding them at nearby Westmoor Park. Abruptly I wail – a huge sound that bursts out. The geese honk back, flapping their wings. I alarm them, frighten myself. The pain is awful and I can't do anything except ride it out. My chest hurts with heaving. And it feels good too.

"Oh, Kristina," I gasp and look up at the cloudy sky. "How can you not be here? The world is awful without you." I stand there, looking at the water and the geese. Behind me I hear Sting sing, *How fragile we are, how fragile we are.*

22

The first summer Kristina was away at graduate school for several weeks, her cat, Annabelle, needed inoculations and I took her to the veterinarian. At four months, the kitten seems manageable so I'm unprepared for her wild reaction during the exam. She turns into a hissing, frightened fury. Quickly the vet hands me a pink towel from the carrying case to wrap around Annabelle, hug her, and hold her still. The vet and assistant put on what look like the type of gloves bird handlers use for eagles and hawks, covered up to the elbow. I hold the little fur ball while they examine and inject her under the towel. I soothe and cuddle, trying to help. I feel her racing heart. After a short while her panting slows and she relaxes slightly.

Six months later Annabelle is back to be spayed. Kristina takes her this time and tells us it was an even greater disaster. "She was awful. Soooo scared. I couldn't calm her down and she got out of the towel we wrapped around her. The vet asked me to back away."

Kristina shakes telling the story. Apparently the cat raced around the exam room, determined to get away. The eagle gloves came out again and they had difficulty catching the strong kitten. Finally, the vet scooped her up and moved her into a cage in the back to wait for the procedure.

"How are you?" I ask.

"I stood there and cried. It isn't her fault she's like this. When I saw her in Boston she was crying and clinging to the cage wires, upside down. I knew I had to rescue her. She just needs love."

"But maybe love won't be enough," I say. "It isn't in her nature to be calm around people or let them pet her."

Kristina is thoughtful. Reluctantly she says, "No ... my friends don't like staying with me either. Annabelle claws and nips. They're afraid she'll attack when they sleep."

"Has she ever?"

"No, but one morning Jen woke up with Annabelle sitting on her chest, staring at her. She was afraid to move until the cat left."

"Good plan," I murmur.

After three more years, there is another visit to the vet. Kristina arrives home bleeding from multiple claw and bite wounds.

"This last visit was the worst," Kristina tells me over the phone. "Annabelle has a heart murmur. The medicine is so expensive and only comes in drops. Like I could even hold her to give them to her."

"Honey, we'll help pay for the medicine for you if you find a way to give it to her."

"The vet said the condition is mild and Annabelle will have a quality life if she doesn't have the drops, though not a long one. We decided not to do them for now." Her voice sounds discouraged and defeated.

"You're giving her a wonderful home. Don't let this get to you. She's a lucky cat to have you to love and care for her."

When Kristina was away, her cat was semi-sociable with Bill or me, lounging close by and relaxed. Sadly, the post-suicide Annabelle is not the same. After Kristina's death she becomes hostile and starts attacking strangers. When our realtor is at the condo to sign papers, Annabelle leaps onto the dining table and lunges for Jackie's face with her paw raised and claws extended. Bill barely blocks the attack in time.

The vet thinks the cat is traumatized by seeing Kristina die, behaving as if she knows she's left behind, that her special person will not return. The doctor cautions us about risks to others now that the condo is on the market. The wild look returns in Annabelle's eyes when I stop by and she is distant, loses her appetite, huddles in one place, lashes out at me now when I reach out soothingly.

I contacted several friends and one no-kill rescue center. Unfortunately, they consider the cat a danger and not adoptable. As Annabelle declines the advice is now to put her to sleep.

"Yes, Mrs. Stahl, we make house calls," the vet tells me, "You're doing the right thing."

By the time the vet and her assistant come to the door of the condo I had managed to lure Annabelle into the small bathroom with an open can of food, her last supper.

"You stay out here in the living room. We're going to use this net to keep her still, then sedate her and take her to the office."

"Be careful," I say.

While I wait outside I hear scuffling. Then I hear a cat yowl, a muted version of the tormented sound Annabelle wailed when I looked down on her from the balcony weeks ago. My heart lurches. The scream diminishes to a cry, then soft whimpers, as if she's giving up. I cry too, hold my sides, pace in the living room, and talk out loud to Kristina, telling her how sorry I am that we have to put her pet down, to please forgive me. The bathroom door opens and the vet joins me with an open box. Inside, Annabelle is relaxed and sleeping, panting gently.

"Would you like to say goodbye?" the doctor asks thoughtfully. Her eyes are filled with understanding and sympathy.

"Yes, please." I pet Annabelle softly, long strokes from her pink ears, down her back to her tail, then under her chin. Her all-white fur is soft and warm. I give her a little kiss and murmur goodbye.

"You know, I've never been able to pet her like this before," I whisper. Dr. Lafer nods at me and I realize she probably hasn't either.

23

When I go for my first hair appointment about six weeks after Kristina's death, I am amazed at the change. The top has grown out mostly white. There's still brown hair remaining around the edges, making me look like I have a cap on.

"It's the shock and grief," my hair stylist says. "I've seen it before. Your body triggers the change. Now we'll put color back in. What do you want it to be?"

She is beautiful, petite, energetic and kind. Kristina found Mag and raved about her. They experimented with cuts and color. Kristina always looked fantastic after her visits.

"You should have Mag do your hair. That hairdresser you have makes you look old," Kristina told me.

She rarely came on strong about my appearance, preferring a gentle approach to point out my fashion errors. She'd say, "Hmmm…not your best choice for tonight. Don't you have…?" Her own tastes were simple and practical. Without missing a beat, she'd rummage in my closet for something else.

Now I sit in Mag's chair trying not to cry as I look in the mirror. My skin is blotchy after weeks of daily tears and my eyes are framed by awful, lusterless, grey-white hair. I feel a decade older. All I want is to ask Kristina what she thinks I should do. Our wise daughter was terrific with advice, always sharing her thoughts and opinions about life – music, books, clothes, movies, hair styles, fashion and fun places to go. It's tough going through life without her.

"No more mother-daughter brown color, Mag." I surprise myself saying that. Kristina and I enjoyed years of similarity with our brown hair. Mag looks in the mirror with me, holding up hair swatches by my face, checking for skin tone. We pick a lighter brown for the new normal.

Unfortunately, most of my new normal is not as easy to achieve as hair color. Little actions become big deals, doable only by saying to myself *I will honor Kristina today. I will get up, get dressed, and go to work.* Each movement takes more concentration and time than I ever thought imaginable. Buttons are impossible to fasten. I tremble so badly sometimes that I'm afraid to drive to work. Make it not matter that I want to retreat and give up. I'm not sleeping well. I get up earlier and earlier to allow plenty of time to get ready.

"What time is it?" Bill asks.

"Oh, about 3:45. I need to get ready for work. Go back to sleep," I soothe. It is a measure of his own grief that my early risings seem normal.

Work is all about getting ready, showing up, and being there as if all is well. I am counting on work as the one exception, the one area where I still function. Work becomes essential for my health and future well-being. I invest business with power to stabilize my life. It's where I prove I'm alive; reassure myself that I will go on and survive our daughter's death. I am determined, and work is the way to do it.

So work becomes more important than at any other time of my life. It is the place as well as the activity where I find value and comfort. The thirty minute drive is familiar. The lobby is welcoming. Co-workers are sympathetic and helpful. Business goals are achievable, especially when compared to living each day without Kristina. Work is my comfort zone. Being a professional with familiar routines and supportive associates is completely opposite from how I'm feeling: that I've failed my own daughter.

24

The dawn light begins to creep across the wood floor and nears the sofa where I'm reading yet another self-help book on suicide and loss of a child. I was sleepless at one, then two, then got up at three. I'm completely intimidated by the do-this, do-that lists for successful healing and recovery. There are even not-to-do lists on how to protect myself from more damage. Hah! The worst has happened. How could there be more damage to come?

One of Kristina's friends recommends *Night Falls Fast: Understanding Suicide* by Kay Redfield Jamison. Her words are revelatory. The margins become riddled with my comments and questions. I keep this book close at hand. I sleep better at night. Simply knowing more feels right.

I spend hours on the American Foundation for Suicide Prevention (AFSP) website, which is exceptionally well done. I learn about pre-suicidal conditions of children, teens and young adults that put them at risk, what treatments look promising. I regret I didn't do this before, when she was alive. I berate myself mentally every day for being naïve and content with her verbal reassurances. Why didn't I recognize her mask?

Deep sorrow makes my stomach turn over and over tonight. After yet another trip to the bathroom I wipe my face, hands shaking, and look up at the mirror. My face shows the horror I'm really feeling. I let Kristina down. I underestimated her anxiety, didn't find out more about potential damage. Too late, I learn what I should have grasped before; treatment *must be continued* to maintain a balance with anxiety and depression.

I grieve over these lessons. The next afternoon when I'm driving to

Granby, on an errand, I have to pull off to the side of the road. Regrets again. Sobbing and clutching my jacket tightly I ask out loud, "Kristina, why did you have to go? Couldn't we have fixed this together?"

25

One of Kristina's graduate courses was on Virginia Woolf. I open up a book that includes a character who dies by suicide, *Jacob's Room*, and flip through the pages. Achingly, I recognize Kristina's sharply angled handwriting. She has underlined and starred many sections, written notes, looked up definitions. I imagine her head bent over the paperback, the little electronic dictionary she got for Christmas from Bill one year by her side, writing tiny messages in this book.

One note she wrote on the last page grabs my attention. *Suicide? Please no!* It is written by this section: "'He left everything just as it was,' Bonamy marveled. 'Nothing arranged. All his letters strewn about for anyone to read. What did he expect, did he think he would come back?' he mused, standing in the middle of Jacob's room."

Here I am, similar to Bonamy, standing in Kristina's room, feeling that nothing is different. Yet everything is.

Although I read Virginia Woolf and Sylvia Plath years ago, I didn't understand. Suicide was a theme overarching their words, often forgotten in the beauty. Now I am acutely aware they died by suicide and I look for signs, probe for similarities in their illnesses. I think I see Kristina's symptoms, reread the feelings they wrote about for insight. Overly sensitive, I know, but how else do I learn?

26

"Mrs. Stahl, are you going to be okay?" Sara Feldman whispers and reaches out for my hand in the movie theater.

Younger than Kristina, Sara is the sensitive and kind daughter of a good friend. She has joined her mother, me and three of my friends to see the movie *The Hours*. I've read Michael Cunningham's book. I know Sara and I will be seeing suicide tonight. When these friends heard I was planning to go to the movie, Judy said, "Karin, we'll all go with you. You shouldn't be alone."

We're just about the only viewers in the theater. A box of tissues is handy. I start shaking even before the previews are done. *Can I do this?* Somehow, once the film begins, I'm drawn in deeper and deeper. Watching the screen I feel dread, sadness, hopelessness. I see what builds with depression to make suicide become a very real option. I reach for Sara's hand again, needing to feel her caring a second time. She squeezes back. I feel safer. Connected. Margaret, sitting on my other side, pats my arm. I'm also making noise, worrying them with groans. I pat back, reassuring her I'm okay.

Movies are helping me understand the enigma. I choose films about women. I feel an urge to write thank you notes to Nicole Kidman for *The Hours*, to Gwyneth Paltrow for her performance in *Sylvia*, and to Sandra Bullock for *Divine Secrets of the Ya-Ya Sisterhood*. They portray young women in distress and despair so well that I really do understand my own daughter, her death less of a mystery. But I don't write. I'm too raw to say thanks.

27

I read Kristina's poem "Silent Warrior" over and over, absorbing her struggles. I wage a battle too at the sudden silence and emptiness left by our daughter's death. When she lost her war I began mine.

I've searched through dozens of advice books, then have to stop, feeling I've had enough reading and guidance for now. There are precious few voices of loss and hope that grip me. They educate me, don't tell me what to do. They simply describe "beingness" – how parents live before and after tragedies, what it's like to feel this awful everyday grief, and yet go on to make something more of their lives. I absorb their stories with gratitude, marveling at how articulate they are about the death of a child.

Judy Collins wrote two memoirs sharing the suicide of her son; those move me. I read them in Kristina's room where I go sleepless nights so I don't disturb Bill. I am wrapped in a comforter on the bed. Collins' writing is as flowing and beautiful as her music, and I will be forever grateful for the peace and forgiveness her words and understanding bring.

Nine mothers visit Farmington Library on a book tour for *Beyond Tears: Living After Losing a Child.* They talk about surviving the death of their children. I wasn't sure I could handle being in the same room with that much loss, so I go alone just in case I need to leave. I find they are warm and compassionate, sad and brave, and very helpful by sharing perspectives they gained from the "loss club." I don't want the evening to end.

Not until almost two years after Kristina died do I find the book *A Broken Heart Still Beats*, edited by Anne McCracken and Mary Semel. They compiled more than two hundred writings of loss, pain and solace by well-known authors and public persons whose children died. The literature is stunning and haunting. How little I knew about these famous writers who were parents too, some from centuries ago. How incredibly they write of their despair and heartbreak, using the experience to inform their art, leaving the world a better place thanks to their writing. Their accounts are gifts.

I sob with their words and realize for the first time *it could have been worse*. What if Kristina had been murdered? What if she and I had argued, were angry with each other? What if we hadn't lived our lives with love? How great my guilt and remorse would be, even more than I am feeling now. Yes, incredibly, it could have been worse.

I like writing that raises my spirits by the act of reading. I delve into memoirs, accounts not just of loss, but of discovery and personal growth. I read Sue Monk Kidd's nonfiction and carry *When the Heart Waits* around with me for weeks, only to be replaced by another of her books, *God's Joyful Surprise*.

On the Oprah show, Anderson Cooper discusses losing his brother, Carter, to suicide and writing *Dispatches From the Edge*, weaving world issues in with private loss. Their mother, Gloria Vanderbilt, is in the audience. She isn't just a designer, someone who created a favorite pair of jeans I wore in the '80s. Her child died by suicide too. I feel for them. Carter's death changed their lives and I want to figure out what they did afterward.

When Susan Saint James is interviewed by Tim Russert about the Ebersol family's plane crash and loss of their son, Teddy, I am riveted. Another Oprah show includes the whole family as guests. I have bathrobe snug around me and I'm watching TV – on purpose. I rearranged my work schedule to come home early for this program, to admire this family of survivors, to see how they do it as a family, as individuals.

These are life lessons and I pay attention. I'm not going to spend the rest of my life in Kristina's bathrobe. I *will* find a way to awaken to life again. When friends who are parents say to me, "I don't know how you're doing it; I can't imagine losing my child," I simply think of these public examples, parents and family who share what it's like to help others. I do a self talk, "Karin, you are already imagining their loss and strength. Now, imagine yourself moving beyond your own loss and live it."

28

I need to be still and let God love me.
When this old world starts to push and shove me,
I need to be still and let God love me.

Steve Mitchell's voice rises gently in the hushed church sanctuary, a rich warm tenor that embraces and draws me in.

When Hurricane Andrew struck his community in Florida, destroying homes, separating families and leaving devastation, the Sunday after the disaster Steve sang this beautiful B.J. Thomas song at the Coral Gables church where he was then. Now he sings it for us here in Connecticut. Hearing it sung in our undamaged church, I feel beaten up and weep through every note.

29

The day after Kristina died, our minister suggested Bill and I each write her a letter. That started the ongoing flow of my letters to her. I write everything from short messages to long accounts of days and weeks since she left, descriptions of trips and daily events, memories of times we shared together, questions about her afterlife. Although there is no quick cure for grief, the writing helps me heal over time. I pour my injured heart onto the pages, surprised at what I feel and how much.

I tell Kristina news about her friends, marriages, children they are having, road races, marathons and triathlons they enter in her memory. I pass along what they tell me they remember most about her and hold dear in their hearts. I ask her if she sees us, hope it doesn't make it harder for her. I write her mother-to-daughter, carefully, uncertain how to reach her spirit.

Friday, September 27, 2002

Dear Kristina,

When I was in the guest bedroom this morning I remembered the chest of drawers where I stored some of your childhood things. Your Brownie and Girl Scout sashes are in the bottom drawer along with baby rattles, crafts you made in summer camp, and art work from school. It is filled with you, smells like you.

There is also one of your English writing assignments from 1991, "A Struggle for Independence Behind the Wall of Insecurity." I don't remember this. You wrote twice about being a little perfectionist. Oh, honey, even then you felt pressure and anxiety.

At the end you wrote, "It scares me once in a while to think that this is our only life. To think about death is to think about an unsuccessful life, a life where no true happiness can be found, a

place where we don't want to be."
    I wish I could go back to that time when you were fourteen and help strengthen you from that point on. My beautiful child, I miss you.
        Love,
        Mom

Who was the Kristina I did not know? I keep searching for answers in her own words. I type up her journals, drowning the keyboard in tears. My reward, if that's the right word, is one painful discovery after another. Her journals blast away any hope I'd harbored deep inside that her suicide might have been only impulsive. She spent years writing about her pain and anxiety and years keeping dangerous feelings to herself, not even sharing them with her therapist. The mother in my heart urges, *keep reading.* The rational business woman in my head cautions, *wait … there's pain ahead.* My heart wins and continues to ache as I absorb her hidden life.

I come across an entry made when she was in college and had just broken up with her boyfriend at that time. My recollection of the visit was vivid, one of those important mother-daughter times together. She called one Friday afternoon and asked to come home from Maine for the weekend, something she'd never done before, and never did again. When she came through the front door she started crying hard, hugging me and letting herself be held.

I can't fix this for her. This was one of those moments a parent recognizes instantly. As much as I wanted to ease her pain, heal the rejection, strengthen her, I knew those things were not up to me. She wanted a safe place for her to lick her wounds, to simply be. So, after she arrived, I lit a fire in the fireplace, wrapped her in a woolly throw, and brought her some soup kept hot on the stove waiting for her arrival. A box of tissues was handy just in case.

"Thanks, Mom." She ate and leaned back in her cocoon on the sofa, more relaxed. "I didn't tell you, but my roommate moved out a couple of weeks ago too."

That was news.

"Kate said she didn't like who I'd become, that my boyfriend wasn't good for me."

Kristina's been all alone and lonely in the tiny dorm room that really should have had only one student to begin with.

She talked some more, sharing some of her feelings, but I'm her mother, not her friend. Occasionally, she picked at the woven throw like she did when she was a little girl and concentrating. She gazed into the fire as she spoke, her lovely freckled face reflecting the firelight, etched with the sadness of loss.

"I lose myself in him. I am no longer *me*. Part of who I am gets lost. I feel needy, anxious. Sometimes ... sometimes I just go crazy saying things I regret, clinging ... driving him away. Why can't he change it or stop it when I can't? I knew it was ending long before now."

At the time I simply listened, kept her company, and bore witness as she talked to herself out loud, working through the confusion of feelings and thoughts. Her friends telephoned from school, worried about how suddenly she had left, but she didn't talk long with any of them.

Eventually she quieted. I remember comforting her by saying, "There will come a time, maybe even two years into the future, when you will look at each other and not feel the pain first. You'll move on. Become the person you are going to be. Then give your heart again."

After she returned to school, she gave me a copy of a poem she'd written about the break up. Like an epiphany long in coming, I saw she was a writer who used life as material, describing people and scenes in a lyrical style to her prose, a crisp tone to her poetry. Coming home and talking with me was verbal rehearsal, a way to find out what was in her heart that needed to be given voice.

your promise

breaks my heart
your slow whisper
comes too late
too long after my tears
but I hurt
and I take you back
without a fight
you don't chase
if you lost me
there would be no search
you say quietly
"don't leave me, baby"
how can I push you away
why do you move me so much
why am I so vulnerable
I am strong
without you near

but close I am weak
I need you too much
May 31, 1997

30

In October, almost a month into grief, I slip Kristina's cell phone into my purse, add an envelope that contains a death certificate, and drive to the phone store in a nearby mall. When it's my turn to speak with the service representative I tell him, "I need to close our daughter's cell phone account. She died." It's the first time I've had to say that to someone who doesn't know me, didn't know her. The young man looks up at me, intent but kindly.

"I'm sorry for your loss. Please sit down. When did she die?"

"September 11." I bring out the death certificate to show him for authenticity. "Do we owe any payments on her account?"

"No, Mrs. Stahl." He types on the keyboard, canceling out Kristina's electronic existence. Just that simple.

"May I keep her phone? Would you transfer my cell number to it, keep her stored phone numbers?"

He looks at me sharply. I hasten to explain, "I want to carry her with me a little longer." He nods and ignores the fact that I'm crying. When I leave, I feel I'm holding something very precious.

I decide after that visit to make changes to Kristina's accounts by phone or online instead of in person – the dentist, email account, fitness club, credit cards, etc. I'm reminded of all the moves we made as a family, starting and stopping services. How different this is.

"Hello? I'm calling about an appointment my daughter has for this week."

"What is the name, please?"

"Stahl ... Kristina Stahl."

"One moment. Would you please hold?"

"Yes." I wonder if there is a problem.

"Mrs. Stahl?" Another woman's voice is on the line now. "I'm the office manager for the dental practice. We are so very sorry to hear Kristina has died," she says.

"Thank you."

"She was just lovely, your daughter. She was here for several appointments. This was going to be her last one."

"That's why I called. Does she owe you any payments?"

"Let me check."

I'm put on hold. Soft jazz music comes through the receiver. As I wait I remember something about this dental practice. It's the one that includes Dr. Bierly, the dentist who aided Kristina on the soccer sidelines ten years ago when her braces broke. She must have switched dentists after she was eligible under her own employer's dental plan.

"Sorry to keep you. Your daughter was paid up early September." She hesitates. "You know, everyone in the office really liked her. We're very sorry."

Late in the afternoon I logged onto Kristina's email for the last time. There is only one message received after September 11, from a friend who doesn't know she died, so I send an email that I'm sorry to contact her this way and shock her, but Kristina has died suddenly. I include our phone number. Less than five minutes after I log off the phone rings.

"Mrs. Stahl? This is Suzi." She's crying. "I hadn't called Kristina this summer, just kept in touch with emails. When I saw one from her ... at least I thought it was her ... then read your note ... I couldn't believe it. How did she die?"

"Oh, dear, thank you for calling." This is always going to be the hard part, telling people about her death. "She killed herself, Suzi. She was feeling very anxious and depressed about teaching, much worse than before. None of us realized ... none of us knew." I finish lamely.

"Kristina *loved teaching*. What changed that?"

"We're not exactly sure. She met lots of good teachers at Bread Loaf over the summer. She compared herself to them, didn't feel like she was measuring up. So she started a new classroom management program at school and had push-back from one new student." I stop babbling, worried about too much information too soon. I take a breath and wrap it up. "With her anxiety condition, she lost confidence completely."

Suzi is crying harder now. I keep quiet, letting the story sink in.

"I'd like to come see you. Is this Saturday good? There's something you probably didn't know. Kristina helped me with my own anxiety, so I know a lot about it. I can help you and Mr. Stahl." We hang up after making plans to meet. Here another young woman has suffered too, someone who might explain or describe what it's like to feel as Kristina did.

After her call I stop tying up loose ends, at least for today. Although I am grateful for people doing their jobs well, it hurts to cancel Kristina's services, as if I'm removing all evidence of her presence in life. Even when people are consistently kind to me, I can't handle their being so efficient at deleting all our daughter's accounts.

It is simply too much. I put on Kristina's bathrobe, take two Advil, curl up. Tomorrow I'll find courage again.

31

My scrutiny of Kristina's life isn't very organized, more like upending a purse and sorting through all I'm carrying around in there. There's a jumble in my head too; when I touch a thought I skitter away, come back, poke and probe, pick it up, treat it as potential evidence, focus, and follow the stream of questions that pop out.

One medical perspective I've read is that people are hardwired from birth for a brain chemistry imbalance, including an anxiety disorder. I worry after the fact if I made her more anxious, even hurt her by not knowing this risk potential? It's also possible our actions as parents actually enabled her to live longer by helping her feel secure with us. What isn't clear is how pain could increase so much she withdrew from the world. Our daughter seemed to have a happy childhood. We thought we were careful not to put too much pressure on an only child since we realized early on she was demanding of herself.

Looking back, I see touch points in her life where we might have avoided the downward spiral, times when an intervention and redirection may have helped. Little moments that seemed insignificant at the time, certainly normal, I now want to handle differently to reduce her anxiety.

I recall one scene at home when Kristina was two years old. She was playing and wanted to sit in a grown up chair with her teddy bear. She moved a little foot stool up to the chair, picked up the teddy, and tried to climb up. Over and over she would grab onto the chair arms but teddy would slip down.

"Want help?" I asked.

"No! Do myself," she huffed in reply.

I decided not to interfere but hung around close by, peeking into the living room to watch her progress. I counted six tries before she climbed up and into the chair without letting the teddy go. Her smile was radiant. She hugged the bear, patted him into a spot beside her and clapped her hands. "Good Teddy!" she said, then quickly got up out of the chair and walked away to play somewhere else.

At the time I admired her persistence and drive toward independence. I told the story at dinner with Bill and Kristina there. We clapped, praising her. She beamed and laughed. But, is this how perfectionist tendencies start? Did she grow up focusing on gaining approval from us, then her teachers, and coaches? There are astounding familial and social pressures that occur every day from every direction. She probably felt she had to get things right and be perfect at everything. All that perfectionism.

Bill and I both worked after she was born, traveled occasionally, and needed child care. Unfortunately, that meant programming and scheduling began when our daughter was only a few months old; adults controlled her day, every day. Even when she was sick, it required effort to juggle care. Sometimes Bill and I split our days to share doctor appointments or stay home to care for her.

My mother once remarked that Kristina's nature was "very accommodating" and advised us not to take advantage of that. I thought I knew what she meant and started being careful not to tire Kristina out or attempt too much in the time we were together. As a child, she never complained about driving to and from day care, staying with Nanny Dorothea when we traveled, or being picked up by her grandmother some days when Bill or I would have a work problem. She adapted to our world over and over for years. We were coping as best as we knew how at the time.

What I've learned is anxiety is cumulative and may build over years. I wonder if lack of confidence and low self esteem stem from an over-scheduled life, producing anxiety. Kristina became highly functional and appeared independent, seemingly evidence of coping skills. She was also a natural leader attuned to others, no hint that she was subordinating her own needs. Is a social mask *that* strong?

32

My blood pressure skyrockets. I know because I start using a portable blood pressure pump to track it. By the end of a normal work day, plus a few more hours reading and typing Kristina's writing at home, I look at numbers way too high. One day, just after lunch, I feel so ill I almost faint at my office desk.

"Your blood pressure readings are *what*?" Our family doctor is alarmed when I call him. "Please come into the office – right now."

This kindly physician was Kristina's doctor too. His daughter was a high school student of mine several years ago. When Dr. Blanchard telephoned us two days after Kristina's death, we had a conversation I will never forget. He sounded sad, deeply troubled about her suicide.

"I'm going through her records, looking for something, anything I may have missed. I also telephoned one of my colleagues, a psychiatrist who specializes in suicide."

"Thank you. What did you find?"

I was at home, sitting at the dining room table reading condolence cards and messages. Exhausted from not sleeping, I could barely hold the phone.

"First, you and Bill must know, and believe, there is no fault. No fault, no blame. We don't really understand this suicide illness."

I immediately think, *No fault? Like a car crash? Suicide too?*

"Has there been any history of mental illness or suicide in your families?"

"Yes, both of Kristina's grandmothers had problems. Bill's mother was so anxious at times she stayed inside her house, used Benadryl to calm herself. My mother made a suicide attempt when she was newly divorced and very depressed."

"There's a genetic predisposition for many conditions. We're learning so much more about brain chemistry and evaluating if a child is at risk. Mental health disorders can run in the family. Anxiety may become depression. Was she more anxious than usual?"

"She was stressed out after her graduate school summer, even more than last year. Then she was without an assistant at school to help coach soccer. The start of the new school year was hard work too. But we think there was something more going on, a problem with a student. She lost confidence in herself as a teacher. She worried about losing control."

"Quite a combination. I have a note in the file here that she was counseling with Dr. K. Was she still in treatment with her?" Dr. Blanchard asks.

"Not recently. Her therapist thought Kristina was doing well, agreed she should make an appointment in three to six months, then they'd re-evaluate." I stop and think. The timing for another visit would have been while Kristina was in the summer graduate session, so that follow up visit never happened.

"Was she taking medications?"

"No meds. She and her doctor decided on cognitive behavioral therapy and exercise."

"Kids who are strong and tough, especially athletes, often decline drugs," Dr. Blanchard says. "They try treatment first without meds to see if need them. Maybe medication would have helped, but there's no way of knowing." He is trying to be helpful, make me feel better. I'm not convinced yet and he senses that.

"She was planning to call her therapist. She knew her anxiety was worse again. She just didn't make it a priority." I pause. "I should have made sure she went to an appointment."

"Don't blame yourself. After all, she was twenty five, an adult patient. With suicide, impulsive action is common. There is a line that gets crossed and the patient isn't even aware where it was. The impulse takes over. It is *irreversible*. She lost control."

God, that sounds awful. The tears I've been holding back well up. This conversation aids my understanding; at least I have a better idea what she was facing at the time. What I'm finding out now, or recalling what I didn't pay attention to then, frightens me. I remember when Kristina brought home a brochure from her therapist. Dr. K had given it to her when she explained about SSRIs, selective serotonin re-uptake inhibitors, a class of drugs used for anxiety and depression.

"I'm not diagnosed as depressed right now. My condition is performance anxiety, with a perfectionist compulsive tendency." She told us she'd talked with her doctor about how important vigorous exercise is along with therapy visits. Her athletic conditioning and training would encourage her body to increase serotonin naturally.

"What about brain chemistry longer term?" I knew one young woman on my business team who took meds for inherited chemical imbalances. She told me her family had several generations of depression and emotional conditions.

"Right now the goal Dr. K is helping me with is stress management, becoming less anxious in public and in front of people. You know, when life gets intense."

I look at our daughter thoughtfully. We are sitting on the living room couch, reviewing all the materials from her third visit with the doctor. Kristina likes having a plan, something she can implement and control. She is committed to feeling better about the anxiety that has been a part of her, anxiety that surfaced with standardized testing in high school.

Kristina was evaluated years earlier by a different doctor, an educational psychologist, and given suggestions for managing studies, multiple-choice exams, classroom expectations, and other forms of testing and performance. At that time, when she was sixteen, the doctor didn't think follow up visits, medications or therapies were indicated. Kristina was not considered clinically ill. There was no performance anxiety diagnosis so we must have missed another piece of the puzzle then. This touch point looks like a suicide prevention opportunity.

"What do you want to do about medications?" I must have looked worried about her not taking them because she took my hand before answering.

"I want to do this without drugs. I can do it. I'll see her every two weeks then once a month. She gave me an anxiety workbook and there are assessments. She'll review my scores. My anxiety levels aren't too high yet. I'll train myself for social situations."

"Are there things we did when you were young, or things we're doing now and should stop?"

Kristina looks into my eyes. "You and Dad are who you are and work hard. You do your best with me. We're a small family. Okay, you didn't push, push, push like some parents my friends have. And you praise me. But I'm an only child - it's tough being the only one."

Suddenly I'm aware it's very quiet in the house. I hear my breathing along with the ticking of the clock on the shelf, the tinkle of the wind chimes outside on the patio, and the soft snores from our sleeping cat nearby.

"I'm sorry it's been so hard. I didn't realize."

"It's okay. Really. Now I have to learn how to relax, be healthy."

"Honey, you've always made good decisions."

"Thanks. Dr. K told me I can start drugs at any time in the future, not a problem." She gives me a hug and smiles. She looks deceptively confident, even strong.

Two years later I find journal entries written during this active treatment time:

> *Just trying to understand some things. Dr. K puts me at ease. Though I do need to ask her what it is I am dealing with. What is this series of fears that leash me?*
>
> ...
>
> *I am alone. But no. There are people who love me. But I am alone – in that independent sense. Stop forcing yourself to do things that please others. Let it go. Let these things go.*

The conversation with her primary care doctor after Kristina's suicide intensifies my search. Her writing is like reading a mystery she is trying to figure out too. She has long dialogues to convince, argue, soothe. And I cry with how alone she sounds.

> *Fear. I am so afraid. Many thoughts. Nothing sensible or rational. Save one rational thought: you are too much of a coward to take your own life. Even that, I want someone else to do.*
>
> ...
>
> *I don't trust myself. I cannot exist...these fallen words; I have slipped; I am slipping. I am afraid to scream. I am trapped. I can't get out of my self. I am locked in here – no one wants someone who is needy. No one wants a coward like me. I am so afraid. I am scared to communicate. I am so self-absorbed that I feel scrutinized upon every glance...I am so ashamed.*
>
> ...
>
> *My whole life is trivial and tedious – it's this thought that I carry with me that signals my suffering. There isn't true suffering within*

me; it is self-fabricated. All of these things; they happen because I create them. This trauma exists by my own heart and wrinkled hands. Shame.

33

The condominium we found for Kristina came with plantation shutters on all the windows except for the back patio sliding doors in the living room. She always kept the shutters closed; not even a little bit of sunlight got through ... another clue I missed. The only window where I saw the shutters partially open was the one over her kitchen sink that looked out onto a garden area. I was visiting her one afternoon, bringing over some food, and I carried the plate into her kitchen. She must have been able to tell I was itching to open the shutters.

"I haven't adjusted to people living so close around me. They come and go on the walks talking. So I keep the shutters closed," she explains.

"Having others close by isn't comforting?" I ask.

"Maybe ... sometimes ... I don't know. I just don't want them looking in."

"Have you had a chance to meet anyone yet?" Next door there is a single woman like Kristina who is an intern in a nearby hospital medical program. Her roof leaked and she'd had to move out for weeks while repairs were being made.

"Yes. When I go out in the morning for work and walk down to the parking garages I talk with the couple in the corner unit. And the guy next door on the left nods to me some nights passing on the walk. He's the one who plays loud music, lots of bass. It sounds threatening some times."

Threatening? Not a usual word.

"Do you feel safe here, honey?"

"It's not the same as the apartment over the office."

34

"Hi, Kristina. It's nice to see you," our lawyer says, shaking her hand. Then Bill, Kristina and I join him in the conference room at his legal office.

Mark has a warm smile. He worked with Bill and me to set up a trust, complete first-to-die insurance applications, document possessions, and revise our wills. One step was to ask Kristina if she would agree to be a co-trustee. When I telephoned her at graduate school and told her about the arrangements, I asked her to join us for a meeting with the attorney when she was next home.

"I guess so, it's just I don't want to think of your dying before me." I could hear Kristina's voice in the dorm hallway, quiet and soft, but troubled. "I mean, I don't want to lose you." I hear her light intake of breath and am kicking myself for asking her over the phone. Now I could tell from her worried voice, I made a mistake.

"We don't mean to upset you. I'm so sorry I brought this up now. We'll do this another time. Don't worry."

"No, it's okay. You know how I am, the only child thing again. I'll be all right. You and Dad make the appointment and I'll do whatever adult thing that's needed." She sounds resolved now, less wary.

The legal office is a mix of formal and artistic with an art gallery look. Large pastels grace the conference room with bright splashes of farmland, barns and forsythia. Kristina sits next to Bill and I'm directly across the table. Mark addresses Kristina as the prospective co-trustee during the review of the various trust provisions. At first she asks a few questions and reads through a few sections Mark points out to her.

Even though the room is ventilated there are no windows and I see Kristina beginning to pale. Her lip trembles and she looks shaky.

"Are you all right?" I ask.

She looks at me, then Bill. "This is hard," she whispers.

This now looks like a very big mistake. Kristina listens intently as Mark speaks, but I know she's absorbing the notion we'll die one day. Up until this point, she and her friends probably haven't ever talked about their parents' estates or wills before. The trust documents we're going through outline responsibilities, accounting, legal follow up, and estate actions. Very daunting...and too much for her condition.

"If, for any reason, you want to resign as a co-trustee, that will be arranged," Mark adds.

"I'll be fine. I want to do this," she says. Kristina glances over to Bill and he quickly puts his arm around her shoulders for a bracing hug.

"Thanks, bud," he says.

When I was a teenager, traveling with an exchange program in New Zealand, I remember being in an earthquake there. The force of it threw me to my knees. I gripped the floor as things tumbled around me. It happened so fast, no warning, and then the earth movement stopped as suddenly as it began. I now think the timing of our trust action probably created the equivalent of an earthquake for Kristina, tipping the mental balance into suicidal thoughts.

35

I've been back to work at Kaiser Permanente for a month and am going on a business trip to the home office in California. What an appropriate state to travel to, since it feels like there was a huge earthquake in my life and the aftershocks are ongoing, all the time, everywhere I go. The tectonic plates of my life are askew and rearranged, constantly shifting.

Each step is new and I absolutely don't want to take many more. I just want to go back to how I felt and lived before. In the aftermath, my professional friends grieving with me ask, "How is it going?" or "What can I do to help?" and they really listen for an answer. The people I work with know I need help to move forward through this twisted new terrain.

Fear grips me while I pack, insidious and constant in my belly. It follows me when I drive to the airport, shuttle to the terminal, unload at the check-in counter. I shake just standing in line. This is not normal for me; I usually enjoy traveling and feel confident.

"Your flight leaves from Concourse B," the airline representative tells me as she hands back my ticket and baggage check. I nod and move away from the high counter. Going through security I don't look around and people-watch as I used to do. I stare straight ahead and move up, inch by inch. This new frightened feeling is deeply visceral. Nausea comes as I lift my laptop to the rollers, take off my shoes, and walk through the screening arch. This grief makes me feel cowardly. I'm practically broadcasting a message – *my child is dead and I can hardly walk.*

Yet I do walk, at least as far as the departure gate. I'm not engaging with any people or surroundings. Timid mouse. I see John, Jean and Carrie standing by the window. I smile, recognizing my colleagues, and I'm grateful. I need shepherding. It's crowded and I weave in and out, careful of feet, bags, and a toddler pushing her stroller with a watchful mother beside her.

"You made it. You're here." John gives me a quick hug. He has such sympathy in his eyes and assurance I'll make it, and those feelings give me confidence.

After one plane change in Chicago and seven hours in flight, we're finally all in baggage claim at the Oakland airport. "That looks like your bag," he says, bringing me back into focus. I'm mesmerized by the bags going round and round on the carousel, not registering which one is my own. Paying attention takes such energy.

"Right. Thanks." I'm grateful for his courtesy. Hearing my own voice is a bit of a surprise. I sound normal considering all the grieving thoughts on overdrive that kept coming at me on the plane, even when I tried to read the pre-meeting material. I finally gave up and closed my eyes.

"That's a small bag," Carrie says. "You must be an efficient packer."

"I don't plan to go to the evening dinners and social events," I explain. "My energy level doesn't last beyond four in the afternoon these days."

When we arrive at the hotel, several Kaiser friends linger in the lobby. "You're looking well," Nancy remarks. A warm hug accompanies her words. "We're all glad you decided to come to the National Accounts meeting."

I gulp and hug back. In a few hours, prior to the beginning of the meeting, there is something Nancy and I will do together. There is going to be a memorial service for one of our Kaiser friends who died about six weeks ago, just after Kristina.. I agreed to speak about my friend Tucker, and Nancy has generously offered to stand up with me, to step in and read if needed.

Tucker had cancer and returned to Connecticut for hospice care, wanting to be near her parents and the home where she grew up. Once, after I'd come back from a hospital visit nearby in Middletown, Kristina and I went out to dinner together and I shared with her my admiration for Tucker's courage and sense of humor in the midst of her terminal illness.

"She's quite an example, isn't she?" Kristina asks as she looks at me closely. "You okay, Mommy?"

"No ... I'm going to miss her when she goes, honey. This is hard, being there for someone as they die."

"Shhh, shhh. It's okay," she says and leans over the table to hug me.

Hard to believe Kristina died before Tucker, suddenly, and with no obvious warning. One day I visited Tucker in the hospital and the next week a Kaiser friend took my place, telling Tucker my daughter had died and I wouldn't be able to come to the hospital for a while. So the upcoming memorial service in California is important to me. I never saw Tucker again, never said goodbye.

Two years after the trip, when I weed office files before retiring, I read emails and reports I prepared during the first few months after Kristina died. There are notes from this October 2002 meeting and I have absolutely no memory of writing them. There is a copy of the memorial address for Tucker as well. No recollection there either.

Perhaps this lack of memory was a temporary disability, a condition I passed through; like the bags on the airport carousel, someone was there to point mine out and help me keep moving.

October 29, 2002

Kristina dear,

This is the first trip I've made away from home in twenty-five years that I don't have you to come home to. It feels awful. A shock. A sense that the world you, Dad and I had together is completely out of kilter, off balance.

I remember telling people, "My daughter is my reward at the end of the work day." I would rush to your day care from work to see you, go home together to cook for you, read bedtime stories, hear your school news, watch sports, review homework – all those wonderful activities with you that enriched our lives.

This pain does not end. There isn't anything you can do about it where you are now, at least not that I understand. Can you join God to help give me strength to bear this loss? My faith in you is great; perhaps I believed in you too much and wasn't alert enough to your anxiety and anguish. Oh honey, to turn back time would be so wonderful!

Love,
Mom

36

Dreams come, waking me, depleting the little store of energy I guard. I try to create a calm relaxed bedroom at home, or when I travel, using candles, favorite music, and photos, an environment where I emotionally and physically recharge. But it makes no difference where I am, at home or away, I can't outrun the dreams. Kristina once wrote, "Funny how dreams mirror the passing of life."

When the first rescue dream awakens me, I struggle to keep from yelling with joy. I got to Kristina in time! A true rescue. Tragedy was averted, lives restored, and everything got back to normal. I wake up jubilant, so certain rescue is the reality and her death only a nightmare.

Night after night I create more rescue opportunities. The details of the recurring dreams vary. They are always vivid and clear. The scenes play out in high-definition as I act in a carefully scripted film. There is a voice from an unseen director to guide me and there are several takes to get the rescues right.

"No, that doesn't work. Try it again. Come in the front door of her condo. Use your own key this time. You wouldn't stop to knock or ring the bell if you fear for her life. Right? Hurry into the living room. Stop. Then look up to the balcony. Got it?"

My hands shake holding the key. This isn't acting. I really feel bone-deep terror for my daughter. I tell myself to calm down, there is enough time to save her. Somehow I know she will be on the phone for at least five more minutes, enough to stop the suicidal impulse.

"Action!"

The scene starts. I'm in the car. I've parked in my usual spot in the parking lot. I shut off the car engine, remove the car key. I search in my handbag to find Kristina's key for the condo. It's out and ready in my

97

hand this time as I race from the parking lot. It's about 9:30 p.m., only minutes after she called me at home. The drive takes three minutes door to door, so I'm here in time and the rescue begins.

Clutching her key, I dash down the sidewalk leading up to her front door. Details fill the dream – soft lighting lines the path, rhododendrons grow along the walls, late season cicadas sound. I arrive at the door, insert the key into the lock. No doorbell this time, I push open the door and call out to her, "Kristina!" Surely she has not died in those few minutes since I spoke with her?

"Mom? Is that you?"

Her worried face appears from the dining room. She has the phone in her hand. Thank God. I've interrupted her last call to Chris. I feel like shouting with joy that she is alive and still on the phone.

"I'll call you back. Mom's here," she tells Chris.

Kristina walks over to me, irritated by my appearance. "What are you doing here?"

I manage a shaky half-laugh, half choke. Better to have her outrage than her death. As the rescue scene continues, I keep doing everything right and the director lets the action unfold without stop. I walk close to her, smile, and pull her into a careful hug, not fierce or clingy, nothing that will scare her. My embrace is motherly and soothing, protective but not too tight. Inside, I want to squeeze and hold on forever. Outside, I am content to hug lightly and calm her. "I need a hug," I manage to whisper. "I worried about you after we talked."

"Cut," yells the director. "Good rescue!" The scene complete, this dream ends here. Fade to black. Wake in anguish.

After a month of these dreams, the scenes stop being rescues. They take on a dark and frightening tone, malevolent and ugly, true nightmares. I awake drained and horrified. There is lingering darkness. No more vivid colors, there are shadows everywhere.

One dream frightens me especially and I discuss it with a professional. It's a dream of war, set in Eastern Europe, perhaps Bosnia. Kristina and I are part of a resistance effort. We're separated. I'm caught running in a field and brought back to a makeshift headquarters. Kristina is captured too and is tied to a post several yards in front of me. She does not look tortured or in pain. She smiles sweetly when she sees me, apparently without distress. There is a resigned, peaceful, and forgiving expression on her face. She is light in this dark scene.

A military officer dressed in fatigues stands next to me in the dream. He shows me two bullets, one brass cartridge and one white. He explains the white bullet is a blank, the brass one is real. He loads a pistol with both bullets and hands it to me. He tells me to shoot my daughter.

This dream has three endings:

In the first ending I refuse. The officer raises his own pistol and shoots her anyway as I watch in horror.

Second ending, I shoot her from a distance. I can tell from her facial expression she knows what I am doing, that my shooting her means she will not feel terror from someone else killing her. She does not want to see me die first, something I sense instinctively. The bullet is the real one and she dies by my hand pulling the trigger.

In the third ending, I walk up to Kristina and hold her close, even though she is tied to the post and cannot hug me back. I tell her I have two bullets, one for her and one for me, and then I shoot her. I open the chamber and look inside, see only the white bullet left. *Now, how am I going to die and join her?*

When I described this terrifying dream to the counselor she said, "Dreams have many levels. Usually death symbolizes transformation."

She has a soft face, clouds of dark curly hair, brown eyes. Her voice is soothing. "Not only is Kristina already on her path of transformation, you are too. What do you feel after these recent dreams?" she asks.

"I'm terrified. No matter how hard I try, they end badly and I kill my daughter. Kristina always dies."

"Your dreams are bringing you closer to acceptance. They're part of your grief journey."

She stops at this point to give me a breather, walks over to a teapot and pours me a cup of herbal tea. My hands shake, accepting the cup. I feel cold. She resumes her seat across from me in a brown leather chair.

"Do not fear the dreams; they reveal where you are."

"So where, exactly, am I?" I ask.

"You feel guilt," a statement, not a question. I nod.

"I feel it's my fault. She got worse because I didn't learn enough about anxiety, the threat. I could have saved her life and I didn't."

"Was that your job?"

I look at her, trying to figure out what she means by the question. I'm puzzled.

"Isn't it the parent's job to protect their children – the most important job they have?"

"She was an adult."

"She wasn't able to act like an adult. She was sick."

"What else?"

"She needed me to get her back to her doctor for more treatment and I didn't do that," I continue.

"I know you think you could have made the difference here, a life-saving difference. But no one saw it coming, not you, not anyone."

"That's why I'm the one who should have. I'm her mother. I had a last phone call and there was still time to save her." I bend over at this admission. This hurts so much reliving failure over and over again.

"Your dreams are telling you something. Neither you nor Kristina are in control in the dreams. No more than you were, or are now, in real life."

Nightly traumas diminish after this session and I gain a reprieve in sleep. I must be accepting her death because my dreams become less painful, snapshots instead of long, drawn out terrors. They change into brief visitations from Kristina, a positive indication of where I am in the healing process, rich in details. The normally robust terrain of sensory experience in my dreams that I had before Kristina died returns. Smell, sound, color, texture and light increase. The heart-wrenching rescues are replaced by memories of our life together or entirely new situations where I recognize she's already dead.

In one new dream, Kristina and I are camping together in the woods. There are no other people, just the two of us. There are tall pine trees. Light filters through the branches. It is shady and cool. The ground has a soft cushion of pine needles. Gentle, non-threatening atmosphere. No sounds of animals, any birds or movement other than our walking in the grove. We walk toward camp gear piled on the ground. There is no tent set up yet, just duffel bags and bed rolls heaped together. She and I do not talk as we walk. We do not look at each other. I am directly behind her. A cell phone rings and my daughter kneels, searches in one of the duffel bags. She locates the ringing phone but does not answer it. As she looks at the number on the cell phone in her hand she says, "I don't know why people are calling me. Don't they know I'm dead?"

In another short dream there is a gift. I can't tell whether it's a present for Bill or for me, so I assume it's for both of us. The box is wrapped in gold paper with a white ribbon. The tag is in Kristina's handwriting, *Love, Kristina*. After I read the tag I wonder how this can be when she's dead. I wake up before opening the gift.

At ten months of grieving there are two especially memorable dreams. In the first, it is early morning and Kristina comes to stand by my side of our bed. We are at our old house in West Hartford. She is young, about three years old, dressed in a long flannel nightgown, so it is probably fall or winter. She has her tattered and beloved yellow blankie with her and is sucking her thumb quietly.

I blink away my sleepiness and say, "Hi, honey."

She tells me, "I had a bad dream."

I scoot over to the middle of the bed, lift the covers, and she crawls in, nestling with me and the cat, Sheldon, who crawls up from my feet where he was sleeping. It's a sweet tender moment. I don't ask what her dream was about, I just hold her to make it go away.

The second dream comes from a memory. We're shopping for clogs and a fall outfit for her. In real life, I'd received her last thank you note for the clothes we found for her only days before she died. In this dream she is tired, her eyes downcast. I want to gather her in my arms and hold her safely from harm, for I know what is to come. I dread it; feel great sadness along with helplessness to stop it. I am unable to stop her fear too. I am rooted in a spot outside the store. She hugs me and says good bye, tells me she has more work to do that afternoon back at school to get ready for when classes start. In the dream, as in life, we simply part.

"I've got to get back, Mom. I'll call you and Dad this weekend."

After waking up I regret again not following her to school, doing something as simple as quietly reading by her side while she worked in her office, then have her call her doctor, get help – anything but waking to this here and now.

37

Our grief is new and raw. Bill and I are headed to a support group meeting for people with loved ones who died by suicide. It's called Safe Place, a name immediately resonant with me because in our daughter's goodbye letter she had written *I must find somewhere safe to be*. So do we.

There are about eight people here. The meeting is in a church community room, sparsely furnished with chairs, sofas, coffee tables. In the back of the room there is a small table set up with coffee and tea, ice water and some cookies. To the left, there is another table that has several books spread out. I recognize some of the titles from my readings on suicide.

"Hi. Are you Karin and Bill? We spoke on the phone."

A pleasant, brown-haired woman comes up to us and we shake hands. It turns out she and her husband are survivors themselves and started the group seven years ago after their seventeen year old son took his life. She has us fill out name tags and then introduces us to others standing close by.

"Your first time?" a woman asks. We nod. "Why don't you sit here, by me," she says and guides us to a long sofa.

"All right everyone, let's get started," tonight's leader says.

"Remember that everything we say here is voluntary and confidential. You may speak or pass, it's up to you. We'll go around twice. Start by telling us the name of your loved one, when he or she died, and how."

The meetings begin this same way each month. These are people like us – mixed ages, parents, siblings, relatives, friends, lovers – all grieving and learning how to go on. We are combatants, fighting our fears, struggling to understand and cope with suicide. We are often quiet and withdrawn, broken and hurting.

"Our son just came back from a tour of duty in Afghanistan," a mother is saying. "He was so strong for others," her voice fades.

"I knew my husband was down about losing his job and not finding another right away," a wife starts.

"Three years ago my sister was raped. Two days later she killed herself," a teenager tells us. Her mother sits by her side. They look shell-shocked. It is a miracle they are even here, dealing with that level of post traumatic shock.

My turn comes. "Our daughter was twenty five. She was treated for anxiety but it got worse and she believed she was failing at teaching. She hanged herself." I stop, unable to say more than that.

After several meetings I realize how vast the range of feelings. At any given meeting we feel, collectively and simultaneously, bewildered, sad, angry, shocked, and guilty. All the time there is the guilt. We go over details with each other to bear witness and offer support, examine clues that we missed, suggest steps to take now to help others in the family not become suicides, practice responses to make in public about suicide, and offer up anything else that strengthens us until the next month.

Intellectually, I know I am not responsible for my daughter's suicide; emotionally, I don't believe that yet. After several months, I begin to feel drained after the meetings. I dread hearing all the stories. Bill and I have been doing commemorative things such as setting up an educational fund and offering a scholarship in her memory. These actions are different from what the others are sharing.

There's no time period for grief. Regardless of society's expectations that one year about does it, in reality, that's not the case.

There are sometimes similarities, but rarely do we grieve the same way and certainly not in the same amount of time. Loss is complex and healing even more so, linked with our personalities and core nature. We travel this grief road at different speeds. When you see one suicide, that's exactly what it is, one suicide.

It doesn't feel soon to me to do things in her memory. It's the next most necessary thing, as my Jungian friend told me. I've had a crash course, very compressed and intense, in trauma and tragedy, and the key to moving on is to carry on. I'm learning I heal by serving.

I sense I make a few in the group feel uncomfortable, as if I'm going too fast and cheating. No one cheats grief. Many of us are doing inner work of spirit - reading, writing, and counseling – not visible public things.

A group isn't always a fit for survivors' needs. Bill and Chris didn't return after the first meeting. After almost a year, I find I no longer want to be part of any group. Although I've been helped and want to give back in return, I don't want to talk about grief. I want to talk about living. I'm afraid I'll get stuck, no longer willing to solve her mystery, make changes in life, content to simply tell the story of her death, bear witness to her life; but that means not living my own. That scares me.

38

An acquaintance of mine makes her way over to me in a coffee shop. From her expression I know she wants to talk.

This happens to be one of those mornings when I'd prefer to shuffle through the line with my head down, engage in no eye contact, and hover below the radar. Instantly on guard, I nod in return to her slight wave, feeling defensive instead of open. I stall by sipping coffee until she reaches me. Her words are very direct.

"I've been wanting to ask you about suicide." I look into her eyes. There's a seeking there, a true need to know something. I recall she has two sons.

She continues, "This could have been any one of us. I don't have a clue what's going on in my sons' lives. Now I'm scared about that."

If there is one common theme among all our friends who have children, it is the worry this will happen to them. Their worlds turned upside down too when Kristina died. They knew her, saw no illness. Bill and I are treated cautiously now, marginally approachable. On the other hand, after this happened to us, we became a potential source for knowledge about their own children and how to prevent it from happening to them.

When asked about our daughter's suicide I usually say, "Our daughter had a mental condition. I didn't see the threat."

This is so hard to say. I don't forgive myself for not being more informed about her condition and treatment. I don't want any parent to feel the same way. So the advice I offer is to be very present in their children's lives, listen and ask how they feel about things. Offer medical care and ask for details.

I've imagined what it must have been like for our daughter to be in constant mental anguish toward the end, feeling powerless and unable to ask for help. I've tried to figure out at what point suicide became the option, a very real choice. She didn't think she even had an alternative at that point and was out of other options. Our daughter did not kill herself intentionally to hurt us, of that I'm deeply certain. She just didn't see any other way to stop hurting.

One day, when she'd come back from a therapy session, Kristina told me, "I hate being out of control, Mom."

How I regret not seeing her admission then as a suicide clue. I look back and see how the emotions of her condition swamped her in the classroom, robbed her of sleep, eroded confidence and her ability to cope or love the broken spots along with her strengths.

Two journal entries made during Kristina's last six months seem the most telling about how her condition was worsening without our knowing. She refers to herself as "she" and is disassociated:

I'm so trapped within myself that I don't even know who she is. I don't have the confidence (or is it desire?) to identify her and stand up for her.

...

There is a great sense of doom within. It is an ever-present feeling...these moments of anxiety fueled by a terrible pressure to control something uncontrollable.

39

After Kristina returns from the summer graduate session in 2002, she talks about calling her therapist, but never does. We think it took too much energy at that point. She probably thought she could handle the accumulating anxiety by throwing herself into getting ready for school. One night Bill answers the phone.

"Nice of you to call, bud," Bill says. I see him smiling and nodding while holding the receiver and listening to what she has to say. Then a little frown creases his forehead.

"The grades you just got are great. This is graduate work at Middlebury. An A and A- are incredible grades! You took hard courses this summer." Another long pause.

"You're too hard on yourself. Professors didn't feel sorry for you." He listens some more.

Then their conversation changes tone, starts up again, this time about how things were at the school soccer camp, a normal tone to his voice now on this end. When Bill says goodbye and hangs up, he turns to me with a worried expression.

"She never thinks she's doing well enough, you know? And she was studying James Joyce." There is genuine puzzlement in his comment.

We saw Kristina reading on the jet to and from Charleston in June just before the summer classes started, pouring through a *Ulysses* volume three inches thick, frequently referencing both a dictionary and a book of explications on Joyce's writings. I sit in the airplane seat next to her reading *The Secret Life of Bees* by Sue Monk Kidd, a writer Kristina met through Chris' mother. Kidd has also been to Bread Loaf. Every so often Kristina looks over at me reading.

"Looks better than my book. What's happening now?" and I fill her in on some of the plot. Then she heaves a sigh and returns to Joyce, diligently plodding through.

40

Clues to Kristina's distress come to me out of order. One day I'm recalling something from her teens. Then the next memory is of her as a grown woman. It's as if I'm a scanning program on a computer, trying to turn up corrupted files, going through everything all the time simultaneously, suddenly stopping to bring a conversation or action to light, to examine it from the vantage point of a suicide clue.

"Mom, I have an idea for school, something I've been thinking about. How about I show you now?"

It's the weekend before faculty meetings start and teachers return to arrange classrooms. Kristina's voice sounds eager, excited about her new idea.

"Sure, honey. Come on over. Have you had any lunch yet?"

I hear the smile in her voice when she patiently answers, "It's two o'clock you know." Teasing and happy sounding, less tired than earlier in the week when we went shopping.

My worry radar switches off. It seems only a few minutes after we'd hung up and I hear her Jeep pull into the gravel driveway. I look out the kitchen window. The late summer day is hot and muggy. The drying bushes in the beds look like they're straining toward shade from the house overhang. Bumble bees hover around the patch of black-eyed susans. Kristina is dressed in a tank top, running shorts, and flip flops. She has a file folder and car keys in hand when she steps out of the car, shuts the door, and looks up at me. She smiles and waves, bright and happy. As she walks to the front door I cross the room and get there just before she reaches for the handle. I pull her into a quick hug, feeling joy at her impromptu visit.

"I'm so glad you're back from school. It's seemed like a long summer." As we move into the kitchen together I chatter on. "How's conditioning going?"

"Today was seven miles. I've got to be ready for thirteen miles in October with Allison."

We move over to the kitchen table. The sun catches on the bird feeders outside; they're close enough to the house and window to see little seeds drop from birdie beaks. Bright yellow, green and ruby finches, along with chickadees, flit from bar to bar, chirping and pecking away. We watch a little more, then Kristina turns to me and opens up her folder. I notice she has a book with her as well.

"I was talking with my roommate, Amy, about her teaching. She told me about a great book." I look at the title, *The First Days of School*. "Amy was named Teacher of the Year at her elementary school and did lots of things recommended in this book." Kristina then passes me a few typed sheets that look like forms.

"Anyway, this is a performance contract for my classroom. The student, parent and I will all sign off and agree to the expectations listed." She waits as I read. She tells me how this plan means no one will be surprised if she calls a parent about students missing homework assignments three times, not respecting classmates, or not following school guidelines in their handbook.

I've been looking at her face as she walks me through. She doesn't look at me, just the paper. Although her words sound confident, she isn't exactly sure about having to do this. I was a teacher for a few years, so I'm familiar with the performance contracting process. I also remember hearing about students rejecting it outright, or their parents, wary of signing anything.

"Is this voluntary?" I ask.

"Well ... no. It's a standard for everyone."

"What if the student or parent doesn't think it's necessary?"

"Why wouldn't they want to agree to homework and good behavior in class?" She looks up at me, clearly disturbed that I raised the idea of people objecting.

"What I mean is, in private schools aren't these expectations givens? Don't you already call parents?"

"It's not the same as when you taught high school years ago," she says. I see I've touched a nerve and regret bringing parents up. "My teacher friends tell me parents call and yell at *them* for kids not doing homework or getting good grades. Like it's the teacher's fault."

She's upset now, really anxious. Too late I say, "I'm sorry. I'm really on your side. I remember how hard it is to have discipline and get the topics covered too."

She's getting up to leave. "I've got to do *something* this year. Or it's just going to be worse than before."

"Worse? You've been getting wonderful feedback about your teaching. You probably don't need to change anything at all." Not sure what else to say, I pause.

"It's done, okay. I've already copied these for the first day. It's in the book and Amy did it. I'm going to start out right this year."

She takes a deep breath. She is close to tears and closes her eyes, getting control of herself. When she opens them to look at me I see her frustration and hurt. "I didn't share this with you to make any changes at this point," she explains. "It's just something I've got to do to make a difference for me in my classes."

"I'm sorry. I didn't understand." I still don't, not completely, but I don't say anything else. I disappointed and wounded her with my reaction to the effort she'd made to gain control of her own classroom. I step over and give her a hug. She relaxes a little into my arms. I say firmly, "You're a wonderful teacher, you know. Everyone says so, not just me being your mother."

Kristina doesn't answer. I pull back and look at her, worried now. "You do know that, right? High school is a tough time – kids, teachers, parents – no one thinks it's all up to you."

"No one's interested in reading books or doing vocab. All they want are their cell phones, shopping, clothes, hanging out, hooking up, drinking," she says.

I rub her arms up and down in a light caress. "I'm sure it feels like that some days. You have students who respect you, players too. They listen. They care."

"I love you, Mom. Don't worry. I'm going to do this and do a better job this year. Oh, tell Dad I got his message about Colby soccer. I'll see you both at dinner tomorrow night."

She moves quickly out the door, gets into her car, waving as usual out the window and tooting the horn as she leaves. I stand on the brick steps, left with disturbing feelings.

Her phone calls and emails to us the two or three days before her death give us no warning of crisis or suicide, at least none that we are aware of at that time. Now, I think about that kitchen conversation. It was fear driving her to find a way to control her performance anxiety and panic about going back into the classroom for another year of teaching. That was another missed clue.

The last email Bill receives from her at work is an invitation to a cookout Saturday. Hard to believe she'd be making future plans like that, but maybe she was deliberately masking her intentions. Tuesday night, September 10, is the last telephone conversation we have together:

"Maybe teaching isn't for me," she says. She repeats the story of the student and push-back over performance contracting. He hasn't turned in even one homework assignment.

"Remember when you were a student and asked to change classes?" I offer. "You knew your first teacher's style wasn't a fit for you. Maybe that's happening here? Maybe your class isn't a fit for this student? Maybe he should be reassigned?"

Kristina pauses to consider this, "I'd forgotten about that. Tell Dad he doesn't have to call back tonight. Tomorrow is fine. I'm going to call Chris now. I appreciate your helping with my issues, Mommy. Thank you. I love you."

41

The strain of coaching and sports responsibilities figure in the mystery too. She must be more depleted than any of us realize. She's barely unpacked from Vermont before leaving to assist the Varsity coach with his week-long girls' soccer camp. Then, just before school starts, she learns she has no assistant for her own Junior Varsity team.

Kristina manages the tryouts and coaching alone. Last-minute practice schedules and field changes upset the parents, who call to complain about disrupted car pools. She tells us bits and pieces about all this.

"I promised parents I will personally drive their girls myself so they can make practice."

"That's so hard, honey." When she tells me, we are out running errands at Target, our annual school year stocking up, also a way to give her a treat financially that she will accept. She is proud about her independence. The conversation gets lost in the shopping and unpacking and I don't pick it up later.

A second big stressor at the same time is electrical problems that almost cause a fire at her condo. Kristina calls me about 6:30 a.m. a few days before she dies. "I think someone tried to break into my condo and cut the wires." Her voice is strained.

"Why do you think the wires are cut?"

"There's no electricity downstairs, at least not in the kitchen."

"The wiring's thirty years old. Remember, I'm coming over this morning to meet the electrician while you're at your faculty meeting. He's going to check it all out."

"Oh ... right." Her voice sounds relieved. She's forgotten about the electrician with everything else on her plate, even that I'd arranged to be there too.

"I'll come over now and pick up some coffee for us."

As it turns out, the electrician discovers a meltdown in places in the circuit box. We are incredibly fortunate there was no fire. He puts in an electrical panel, one located inside her kitchen instead of outside in a utility shed. *That should reassure her*, I think.

Then I leave a message on her cell phone that the repairs are made, she'll see a new circuit box panel inside, and the condominium unit is safe now. But Kristina listens to the message and leaves the first faculty meeting of the year in a panic. She calls me from her cell. She tells me I could have been hurt if a fire started before he got there. It was *her* responsibility. She is sobbing into the phone.

"It's okay, honey. Please calm down. Are you driving?"

"No, I'm in the parking lot. I just couldn't stay in that room listening to the speaker. I didn't get much sleep last night. I just can't handle staying."

"You're tired. Everything's going to be all right." Only later do I see that was the wrong thing to say.

The vision I am holding onto is the strong Kristina who loved running with the passion of a natural athlete glorying in her physical strength. Sometimes I'd drive along Route 4 and see her striding up the hill in the opposite direction toward the reservoir. Her legs take the incline in regular movements, smooth and unhurried as she paces herself. I grin at the ease of her strides, uphill no less, and the pleasure she seems to be having. She's intent and smiling slightly.

It doesn't register she is breaking down. I see what we're used to seeing. I see an adult daughter having work problems and I have misplaced faith in her to come shining through like always. What I miss is the anxious woman inside, how worn down simply managing her day-to-day life makes her.

42

When I get back to work after Kristina's death, Jennifer, our Marketing Associate, is simply there, all the time, every day, ready to help. She is almost the same age as our daughter, slender, with average height, dark hair and a stunning smile. Her natural beauty comes with modesty and warmth. She is particularly gentle with me now. One morning she stops at my office door.

"I know you like to play music in your office. Here's an album I got for you that reminds me of your daughter." It's by Diamond Rio and a popular cut from it is *I Believe*. Oh, yes, I love that song.

"Thank you. You don't know how many times I've been driving and hear this on the radio. I always end up crying, but it's a good cry."

The next morning her visit to my office is even more special. "What are you doing about her condo?" she asks. "Want some help packing?"

Bill and I are uncertain about the unit. We originally thought we'd keep it for a while, visit and feel our daughter's presence. However, that desire is looking less and less practical. We agree we don't think managing rentals is a fit for us. There's too little emotional energy to spare and, financially, the condo is doing no good sitting there. We decide to sell and use the money to fund other initiatives at KO and Colby.

So I tell Jennifer, "We're putting it up for sale. I've got to sort through her things, decide what to save or donate."

"Well, how about tomorrow? I'll do it with you. I don't think you want to be alone." Her incredibly generous offer helps me take the next healing step. We make plans to meet around ten the next day. She comes to the condo door with two coffee mugs in hand, ready to get to work.

"How do you feel about having some of her things for yourself?" I ask her. "It will actually feel good, if her clothes fit you, to think of your using them, not a stranger."

We go up to the second floor. I think about Kristina's predominately black urban-professional clothing in her wardrobe, hoping Jennifer needs things like that. "What size shoe do you wear?"

The next three hours we go through every closet and drawer. She has good suggestions on what to keep for myself too and I set those aside on top of an end table. The rest goes either to Jennifer's growing pile on the bed or into bags for donation. She looks wonderful in Kristina's clothes and I find myself smiling, genuinely pleased to see she wants them.

The next stop is the kitchen. I glance at Jennifer and know she's tiring like I am. "How about looking at the appliances, then we'll call it a day. Do you need anything for your apartment?" Happily the microwave finds a new home. This night I write a letter to Kristina:

November 6, 2002

Dearest Kristina,
    Jennifer helped me get ready for move day after we sell your condominium. Colby and school friends will come to pack up the rest. Dad and I hope the clothes, furniture, household items and personal things will share your spirit with people you loved and who loved you.
    The smell of your products brings tears. The sight of the tasteful arrangement of your things makes me want to shut the door and keep it just the way it was when you were here. Your home, your organizing, your nesting – everything you touched and placed just so is special to me. It's so painful to put away your home and your life.
    I hear the breeze in our wind chimes. Your Aunt Ginny says every time I hear them it is your spirit moving. I listen, watch, and pray for you, dear daughter, and miss you with all my heart and soul.
    Love,
    Mom

Move day is about to happen. "Mrs. Stahl, I've heard from Caitlin, Katie, Schieby and Jen. We'll all be there Saturday morning at ten to help you pack up and move out of the condo. Keith and I will have a rental truck for the big things," Shannon explains over the phone. The wave of emotion I'm feeling listening to her voice is strong. I grasp the receiver so hard my hand begins to hurt.

"Mrs. Stahl?" Shannon's voice is worried.

"Sorry. I'm here."

I walk over to the kitchen counter where I have a list of things to do for moving day. Chris, Dave, and Suzi are coming. Two friends of mine from the Kaiser office, Jean and John, will be there too with another truck. "Counting me, we've got six," I say.

"What about Mr. Stahl?"

"He hasn't been able to go into the condo. It's really tough for him. He'll bring lunch, run errands, and make himself useful outside. Okay?"

"Sure. We'll see you then," Shannon concludes our call.

It seems as if Kristina had just moved in a few months ago; now we're putting her condo up for sale. The memories are so vivid. There's a celebratory photo of the three of us standing together by her stairs on closing day on the refrigerator. My forehead touches the photo when I lean over and cry, cradling the phone.

The 70's era condo has an open floor plan and is in a great location near her school and our home. Of course there are drawbacks when we buy it, but we are optimistic about the project: replace the hot water heater, repair the gas heating unit, update all the kitchen appliances, replace the washer and dryer, fix the bathroom exhaust fan, fix the electrical wiring, install at least six new lighting fixtures, and apply fresh paint. We are not daunted. After all, a fixer-upper will be fun as a family, right? We talk together about everything before signing, and Kristina asks Chris to help with the painting. We have a plan!

Our real estate agent surprises Kristina with a gift – a glass champagne bucket and six flutes. The whimsical hand-painted glassware has light purple and lavender flowers. "This is for your first gathering with friends," Jackie tells Kristina. "And don't think you have to use it just for champagne. Any wine tastes wonderful in nice glasses," she added.

Kristina smiles. "Thank you. I know just where to put this set when I move in. Grandpa's cupboard. How about on this wall, with the champagne stuff inside?" she gestures to where we are standing.

I recall the small china cupboard fondly. My father always displayed keepsakes and memorabilia in his office. With many moves to many states, the china cupboard was the one constant. There were awards from his community service with the Rotary, Boy Scouts, YMCA, Shriners, Sons of Norway, and Masons. There were also model cars, troll figures from Norway, mini-flags from countries where he traveled, mining helmets, and things we children and his grandchildren had made for him as presents. It held a delightful array of knick-knacks from his childhood, family and work. Dad would have gotten a kick out of Kristina's things that went into it. There were unmatched wine glasses, at least ten flower vases (her father regularly sent bouquets) and five beer mugs.

Kristina walks around the dining room gesturing to the space she has in mind. "Right here," she grins and motions. "And all this white paint has got to go. Maybe a warm terra cotta?"

Already, with ink barely drying on the closing papers, Kristina is imagining the decorating and the colors she'll use. She wants a blue kitchen, something not too dark or colonial. A light sage color for the stairs, then she imagines a deeper sage tone on the second floor. She looks at us over the balcony above the living room, liking the view and open feeling. She continues talking as she walks into the bedroom. We hear her voice drift out the door; she wants to sleep in yellow, to wake up feeling cheery.

In less than a month Kristina completely transforms the space. We go to lighting centers together to select replacement fixtures. She spends hours holding up paint samples in different lights before making her decisions. Her savings pays for furniture; our money goes into structure, appliances and bathroom repairs.

When Kristina invites me to come shopping, it is another of those precious mother-daughter days. We make the rounds of furniture stores and outlets. She picks a comfy over-stuffed look for her living room in red denim with khaki trim. The dining room table and chairs she selects are Shaker, and her bedroom is country with oak topped, painted sage furniture. The tiny study fills with sports and computer essentials, a small futon and her desk.

By the time she personalizes everything with books, pillows, throws and candles, her home has the feel she wants for herself. Her last touch is to find a leaf-patterned fire screen and matching sconces for above the mantle, romantic yet practical. She waves her checkbook at me, "Pretty skinny now, huh?"

43

I wake up in a sweat. There is no dream wrapped around me to cause this, only a sheet and comforter, tangled and confining. I fight to get out of bed, stand up. Why am I up? I search for a reason for this sense of urgency.

My navy flannel bathrobe hangs on the end bed post. As I slip it on, pushing my shaking arms through the sleeves, no dream images come back, something that always happens for me. Recalling dreams has become a discipline now, a practice that gets better and more accurate over time. Dreams are a compass I use to orient myself to where I am on the grief journey, an indicator as to where I may be going next. Dreams reassure me I'm normal.

In some dreams I simply relive the past as a comfortable home video scene – a birthday party, Christmas, soccer game, new kitten arriving, dinner out, skiing – nights full of happy family times the three of us enjoyed. When I wake from one of those dreams I smile and feel life. I don't weep afterward in frustration or longing; I stay present in the moment and hug the sweet memories and feelings closely, savoring the moment, grateful for the gift of recall. Those dreams are little gifts, small comforts, reminders of Kristina's warmth and love, giggles and hugs that made up our past together.

Another night, another dream. "Isn't this fun?" Kristina's excited voice is in my head. I see her grin. All we do in this dream is swim, eat a hot dog from a stand by the beach, find a seashell or piece of beach glass, wiggle our toes in the sand under an umbrella while waves wash in and out. "These are little blessings, Mom. We can't take them for granted."

So, why was I awake this abruptly, pacing, looking out the windows, watching the moonlight on our flower beds, scanning the edge of the woods? I notice two deer feeding at the far right, a doe and fawn nibbling the spring grass, stepping delicately, occasionally raising their heads – one brown, one dappled – to sniff alertly. It is an arresting combination to watch. I'm completely still. The deer quiet me. Sometimes Kristina called me to ask about the wildlife I'd seen this week – red fox, deer, raccoons, or wild turkeys were the usual answers. When visiting she would stare out the long windows in the backyard, trying to see what I saw, quivering like one of our cats when the bird feeder near the window is full with bright finches. The most she got to see were chipmunks and squirrels. I hear her soft happy laugh at their antics even now in my head.

I stop pacing and sit down in front of those same long windows in front of the patio. I don't feel distress, but something doesn't feel right. A warning? No, I'm not alarmed, only troubled. Then it hits me. Separation. I can't feel her tonight, only her absence. After months of constantly hanging onto every sensory febrile part of her physical and spiritual presence left on this planet, tonight I am feeling nothing. There is even a silence in my head, no little whispered soothing voice saying, "It's okay, Mom," that I attribute miraculously to her. There is simply me, alone in the night world, no Kristina. I am alone.

I feel more alone than at any time since her birth. Always, she was there. Always, I was Kristina's Mommy, a unique and comfortable identity for twenty five years. Now it's gone. I'm only me.

44

Can't sleep again. Writing in my journal: *Was the pain Kristina experienced by living greater than the pain we're all feeling by her dying? Temporary pain, permanent pain. Pain is pain.*

I write until dawn. I sense a core thought I can't get to, an insight eluding me even as I write and write, trying to capture this stage of grief. I reach for words, struggle. By the fifth anniversary of Kristina's death I will have filled six journals. I'm beginning to understand why she had so many herself. The writing has a life of its own.

45

April 2003 is brisk in Maine, weak sun and invigorating breezes. A wonderful day for sports. This is the first trip Bill and I make back to Kristina's college since she died. It feels awful. Everything makes us want to cry. Her former lacrosse teammate, Angela, is setting up a presentation for Kristina's jersey retirement in a ceremony of remembrance. It will also be a celebration of ten years for the Womens Lacrosse program at Colby College.

As I enter the auditorium the huge theater-size screen is filled with a photo of Kristina and her lacrosse teammates. They are smiling, glowing with youth and joy. Music from the Pretenders fills the room. They sing, *Time, where did you go? Why did you leave me here, alone?*

Too much. I have to sit down on one of the steps and hold my hands over my mouth, muffling a moan, rocking on the step. This wave of grief is so physical. When I look up, photo after photo cover the screen – huge beaming faces, fun scenes on the road to and from games, warm moments, hugging teammates – Kristina and her friends flash for a few seconds each. Overwhelming. Touching. So real I could crawl into the pictures, hear their voices. How happy Kristina looks, and healthy, how normal. That can't be the face of suicide. Eight months since her death and I seem no closer to solving the puzzle.

"Mrs. Stahl, are you all right?"

Angela is looking at me from the bottom of the steps. She is medium height with dark blonde hair, trim and attractive. Her smile warms you to the toes. She has worked so hard on every detail, a labor of love.

"It's wonderful. Thank you." I smile, stand up, and finish coming down the stairs to give her a big hug.

"The first time I watched it projected on a big screen was a shock for me too," she says kindly.

"It just hit me that I will never ever see her play lacrosse again," I say this with surprise. I'm still getting used to the notion she's not coming back.

Doors open at the top of the auditorium and people move inside, chatting about the Colby victory. I wipe away tears on my sleeve, a motion so like Kristina used to make that I manage to smile slightly as I scan the crowd for Bill and Coach Heidi Godomsky. They see me and walk down the steps, stopping every now and then to greet people. Bill receives many hugs from Kristina's friends. He comes over to give me a quick hug and kiss, then he and Heidi walk to the podium at the front of the room. After some shuffling, little smiles and waves across the aisles, we all get seated, quiet down, and turn to face the front where they stand.

From my position, front row left, I see all the faces; a few appear apprehensive. Several are crying already, gripping each other's hands. A few coughs. A box of tissue is being passed along the middle aisle. I recognize Kristina's soccer teammates mixed in with lacrosse players. Her boyfriend, Chris, is here too and seated near the back, close to the doors. He will work as Assistant Coach for Colby Women's Soccer this season and is living in Maine now, welcomed into the close-knit group of athletes and coaches. Jess and Jen sit near him up toward the back.

Bill's good friend, Butch White, is here. College sweethearts from the Midwest, Butch and Caren have two sons. The handsome former football player dwarfs his petite wife. They both lean forward now to smile in my direction. I nod and smile back, grateful they are here. At the time of Kristina's death, Butch made a huge effort involving multiple travel changes to cut short his vacation in Colorado and be at Bill's side at the grave.

The lights dim. Bill steps up to welcome everyone, then introduces seven young women who will each speak about being teammates together with Kristina for the years 1996-1999. These women are wonderful. We laugh, cry, and remember together as they give moving tributes to their departed defensive player, the one who always wore signature white cleats, ran like the wind, wrote poems for the team, and thanked departing captains with kind words and gifts of journals.

"Kristina's legacy goes beyond the fact that there are two All-American certificates bearing her name on the wall in my office. It is more than players knowing she was the best defensive player to have competed during my tenure at Colby. It is something more subtle than that," says Coach Godomsky.

"A connection to everyone. That was Kristina as a teammate ... her selflessness, her humility, her quiet understanding of how things had to work to make the engine of the team run correctly. And that is what she brought to the field. Competing *with* her teammates, working towards unity, was always the goal," concludes Kara Marchant.

46

Writing for our church newsletter is nagging at me. I suspect our minister knew it would when he suggested it early on in counseling. He probably knew the thought of having a deadline for submitting copy, a simple business-like action, would motivate me. So, I write quickly and simply from the heart, thinking about it as an update on grief.

Whether sudden loss of a loved one comes through accident, suicide or violence, some days the feelings can be overwhelming. I write how suicide is a decision of impulse, with permanent consequences, how suicide kills more than the person; it kills dreams and hopes for all of us left behind, the little joys in everyday living, the big joys of love and trust. It tests faith and belief.

I share how suicide brings doubt, changes our view of the past and future. Her death defies understanding, strains our hearts; expands them with grief, contracts them with pain. Although suicide is a decision made by one person, the impact is on many others forever.

47

One of the best pieces of advice I receive about Kristina's writing is from her professor, Jennifer Finney Boylan. Bill and I meet with Jenny, members of the Creative Writing Department, and our Development officer, Ave Vinick. We're on campus to endow a fund for writers-in-residence in Kristina's memory. We meet in a beautiful library conference room. There are smells of furniture polish along with paper scents from hundreds of books, floor to ceiling. A bank of windows on one side opens onto the green. Voices float up to the second story where we're sitting.

"What are you doing with her writing?" Jenny asks me at the end of the meeting. I bend over and pick up a canvas bag. Inside are two binders of Kristina's writing that I've collected and typed during the past year. I set them gently, reverently, on top of the table.

"Wow," Jenny whispers. The other professors join in with murmurs.

"She dreamed of being published. There's so much – stories, poems, plays – lots of expository writing from Colby and Middlebury classes. It's been amazing to read."

"I'll help you," she immediately offers.

Her offer is a defining moment. Although the endowment gives us a direction for honoring and remembering Kristina, Jenny gives me a mission.

48

We dread our first Christmas without Kristina. It takes two counseling sessions to talk over what to do. Thanksgiving was excruciating, Bill's birthday followed two days later. We made a big mistake not to plan ahead for the huge emotional onslaught of this time of year.

Christmas shopping completely disorients me when I try it one early December morning. I turn around and leave the mall. What was I thinking? I hope nieces and nephews welcome checks and cards this year. Maybe I'll find presents for my sister and brother online. That would leave gifts for Bill and his parents, the only ones I feel able to handle selecting in person. As for decorations, the idea of putting up a tree, using ornaments Kristina handled, is terrifying. Thank goodness our friend, Mark, brings Rotary wreaths for the outside of the house. At least that gets done.

Bill and I find going out and socializing difficult, rallying only once or twice for dinner with friends. Movies and plays don't work; my attention span is minuscule and I'm close to hyper-ventilating in small crowds. Even a grocery store feels threatening. Classic signs of grief and stress, I'm told, not to worry.

The phone rings. "What are you and Mr. Stahl doing for Christmas this year?" Shannon asks.

"We haven't made any plans except to stay home. We can't even think about getting a tree."

"Well, how about getting a little artificial one? We want to bring you Christmas. I've talked with Katie, Caitlin, Jen, Jess, and Schieby for starters. How about December 22? We've got lots more to call – Allison, Garni, Wheeze, Kelly, Kara and her husband Jeff, Stephanie ... and we'll include Chris and Dave." Her voice is excited. I can tell she's been thinking about this, trying to figure out how we'll help each other through this first Christmas without Kristina.

"You're amazing. We'd love to have everyone. Wait until I tell Bill."

Her call is just what we need. I get a mini-tree, pre-wired with lights, no tears. Bill carries up some boxes of house decorations from the basement and I put up a few things to make it welcoming for the young people. I manage to bake two kinds of Christmas cookies with lots of tears stirred in.

The Saturday they arrive, we have lunch then settle around the fire to visit and catch up on all that's been happening. Some of them came to help pack up her condo in November; some we haven't seen since September. Lots of news to share, including messages from friends who couldn't make the trip.

As a present for each of them, I've collected and typed up a few of Kristina's poems and stories, including one Christmas story, and other writings she gave as presents herself. I pass those around along with a little decorated box that has a candle inside.

"Ooh," they murmur. "This is just like Kristina," Allison says.

A dozen bright heads bend down to begin reading her words. Next, Chris gets up and passes out his presents, CDs he made for everyone with cuts of music Kristina often played. More oohs and aahs of appreciation fill the room.

"Shannon told us you need new ornaments, so we came up with a theme for you – angels," Jess says.

Out come little bags and boxes. Angels, angels, angels – and they are adorable. There is everything from a tall rustic wooden angel to a crystal one seated and holding a heart. There are even LL Bean boy and girl bear angels. "We're a little angel-challenged in Maine," Jen explains.

One angel candle holder has traveled from Guatemala with Garni. Another angel is whimsical and delicate. There are two cat angels. By the time we say goodbye, all the angels hang on the tree and line the mantle. We hope Kristina sees her friends, the real angels, together with us this Christmas. It's the best it can be without her.

49

"The life of the story is not the same as the story of her life." Jenny Boylan is gently teaching me about writing, patient and persistent.

Bill and I are having lunch with her at the Harrasseeket Inn in Freeport, surrounded by stuffed game, birch bark, and hunting scenes – very Maine. I have typed up Kristina's poetry, short stories and essays. I did not discriminate among age-appropriate writing, drafts or completed works. Some are dialogues revealing her fragile mental state. Some are simply word experiments, trying on a mood or emotion through characters. For me, everything is sacred, but that's not what a reader will think.

"Well," Jenny's careful with what she is about to suggest. "Choose the very best for a collection. Keep the title."

Kara Marchant Hooper and her father, Geoffrey Marchant, both graduates of Bread Loaf, learn of the project from me a few weeks later and offer to help select poems from Kristina's body of work. Before I know it I'm organizing her collection into a book, *Silent Warrior: Finding Voice After Suicide.*

A year later and a small self-publication, someone asks for a copy to give to a friend whose son died by suicide, another person knows a teenager at risk, a counselor has teens she feels are suicidal, and a poet hospice volunteer wants to share some of the poems with patients. Kristina's book begins to make its gentle way into lives.

50

Even though two years have passed, I'm unsettled doing well-known familiar tasks, the same old, same old. I'm edgy, expecting something.

When I lose interest in work, that worries me. I have always loved sales and pride myself on long-term customer relationships, some of them lasting decades. Many of my customers and former business associates came to Kristina's memorial service and shared their own concerns as parents afterward at the reception. We were human together.

Work has been rewarding and a rich experience. What's missing now is I no longer feel that fire in the belly, no drive to top last year's numbers, no competitiveness – and I haven't any understanding when or how it happened, it's simply draining away. I feel no need to validate myself through sales, travel, and renewal cycles.

Oddly, I don't feel burnt out, just finished, as if a phase of my life is over and I'm ready to start another. I feel ambivalent about work. I'm beginning to recognize this is a career turning point and very important to pay attention.

"What are you going to do?" Bill asks.

He's concerned. We're having dinner at home, talking as usual about our days, trying to lift each other's spirits by discussing good things, people in common. Then conversation and tension rise to the next level when I introduce this work dilemma.

"Remember how we used to talk about early retirement even before Kristina died?" There it is, I'm saying the R word. "Well, that's what I want, early retirement."

This notion clearly upsets Bill. His facial features rapidly go through grimaces of fear, disappointment, and puzzlement. "But what are you going to do?"

This time the emphasis is impossible to miss. Doing, producing, creating – all verbs that feature strongly in a family with our work ethic. For all the time Bill has known me I've always worked, including going back right after maternity leave. Several of us working moms set up Neighborcare, the West Hartford program enabling children to be cared for at their own schools. Bill knows the level of my professional commitment, at least what it was. I try and explain this deep change.

"I'm not sure yet." The truth is I'm waiting, deep inside my heart. "What I know is the grind of sales is not the work I want to keep doing. After a break I think I'd like consulting."

In addition to changing work, I am determined to stop imagining Kristina returning home with, "Hi Mom," and a smile as she walks through our door or think she'll leave a voice mail, "Hi guys. Love you."

The bargaining stage is over. I used to wake up in disappointment that I wasn't traded in the night, like a baseball team exchange, my death for her life. I would plead and negotiate in prayer: *Take me instead. Please, I've learned my lesson. Can't we have her back now?* I must deliberately and purposefully embrace the pain of this new normal, accept that our daughter was a part of the world and never will be again.

A mother's yearning does not die easily, and I keep her alive in many ways. I'm open to spiritual connection and reach out to her, looking for signs, just as Bill did in the early months. Everywhere, every day, I see sunflowers and dragonflies, hear her favorite songs. I extend my reach, certain she will speak to me if she can, staying alert for any form of messages. I am in a low-level state of tuning in all the time, staying awake and aware for her presence.

51

With time and counseling during the first two years, guilt feelings lessen. I come to better terms with my regrets, imperfections and lack of control.

After reading her journals, I know her condition was worse than any of us knew; even her therapist was not aware of the depth of Kristina's despair. I'm motivated these days to move forward, make a difference in the world, forgive my own lack of life-saving actions in the past, and be present in this very moment.

Bill and I enjoy philanthropy and start to bring more focus and passion to donor ideas, becoming involved in initiatives for education and mental health, connections we think honor Kristina. One of them is an event in 2004, Stahl's Sprint, to raise money for the new Kingswood Oxford Teacher Mentor fund, established to provide teachers with ongoing guidance and support, something Kristina lacked because she didn't have education courses.

Her school and college friends form a committee with us to plan a 5K road race event hosted on the campus. Two West Hartford restaurants provide food and volunteer servers for the picnic after the race. A talented artist, John Beck, donates the signature art for Stahl's Sprint that goes onto posters, flyers, and save-the-date postcards – a glorious sunflower standing strong and open to the light with blue sky in the background. Music, especially Kristina's favorites, enlivens those gathered in the sunny morning.

We all want a celebration of life. Two years earlier we'd been in shock and grief, heartbroken with loss. Stahl's Sprint is a way to get together in joy, combine her passions for sports and teaching, and make a difference with fundraising for an important faculty development program. The day feels good and guilt wasn't invited.

52

Shannon is the first of Kristina's Colby friends to share her wedding plans. "Will you come with me to the bridal fair? My mother needs to stay in New Jersey this weekend."

Fear comes unbidden, surprising me with a huge wave of dread, and I hesitate. "I don't want to put a damper on your happy time. I'm not sure I can make it through the day without crying," I blurt out.

"I'm going to be a little weepy too. We'll miss Kristina together, okay? I think you'd like it at the wedding fair. And I really do need your opinion on some of our choices."

Shannon is so certain, generous, and understanding. She makes it easy to say yes. We've had days and weeks of wonderful conversations together after Kristina died, sharing dreams where she comes to us giggling or simply smiling. Sharing in her wedding plans feels good too.

The Avon, Connecticut location is lovely with its sweeping, curved, two-story staircase opening into the entry lobby. It will make an elegant setting for their reception. Shannon and I spend time in the display rooms looking at flower arrangements, examining wedding cakes (who could imagine so many icings to pick from?) and critically assess tablecloths (seriously, so many textures and patterns). A few times we burst out laughing and Shannon murmurs, "I wish Kristina could see this!" over some whimsy or another. A huge hors d'oeuvre set-up dominates the back porch with little cards in script describing each delicacy we sample.

"I knew they'd have this so I didn't eat much at breakfast," Shannon whispers in confidence.

And so the afternoon goes by as we make our way through the rooms and hallways lined with wedding vendors for music, photographers, videographers, hair stylists, bridal couture designers. We see gifts for attendants, limousine services, and additional locations for rehearsal dinners and brunches. At times it is overwhelming. Most of the day I carry Kristina along with us, good company in a way that isn't sad. This is another step that shows me how much healing has happened. Being with Shannon, doing this, feels normal. We have a wonderful afternoon together, even with the few tears that manage to squeeze through. Feet throbbing, we sit on the lobby love seat and imagine together another wedding as well, what Kristina would pick.

"Blue. Her color for decorations would definitely be blue - the bridesmaid dresses and ribbons," she says.

We imagine something with pearls as a gift for bridesmaids, roses for flowers, a live band, and probably a book of Rilke poems as a guest favor. To top it off, she would honeymoon on a beach with headphones, suntan lotion, and stacks of books beside her.

53

It's June 2004 and Bill leaves for Florida; his mother is dying after many diminishing years of suffering with Alzheimer's. Although I'd heard a new death brings back prior memories and grief for another, I'm shocked that what I feel is not just grief and loss. I have anger again, emotions I thought were over. I feel like kicking, punching, hammering all that rage out, but I don't know how. So I write:

What am I angry about??
– our daughter died
– I didn't save her life
– I feel helpless over Anna Lou's death
– I feel no control over anything in life

54

Anniversaries of the heart are almost impossible, remembrances on Kristina's birthday and day of death especially. Bill and I stumble through the first year of holidays learning what works for us, family and Kristina's friends. Holidays used to be times together to savor, anticipate with Kristina, make lists and plans, shop, and show love for each other. Secrets, giggles, projects, packing – all those innocent and delightful smiles as she'd get into the spirit of the season with us – the hugs and outflow of affection heaped upon our hearts, seemingly unending. Now, holidays, birthdays, and anniversaries are more like trials to be gotten through. People tell us that will change too.

Hard to believe it's been one year when the first anniversary of her death arrives on September 11, 2003, and people join us at the grave for prayers and readings. In some ways the year really has gone by fast. Time is that elusive. There is a wreath of sunflowers for the grave that has a big Colby-blue bow and her name. At the house we're surrounded by vases of sunflowers from her friends and family. Our home is aglow with bright yellow petals, cheerful black centers. The crisp sunflower smell is unique, earthy and not a bit cloying, more a fresh field kind of scent. I half expect to see a bumble bee among the large clown-faced flower heads.

"Wow," Bill says. We hug each other and cry. I write to Kristina this night:

September 11, 2003
Kristina dear,
*   Your love and peace surround us. Dearest daughter, we all felt your presence. Spin left one of her beautiful poems for you,*

*"Compassion." We read your "Affirmations" poem to hear your
own voice speak of loving, liking and respecting yourself.
It was a beautiful day. Although the love we feel for you everywhere wasn't enough to keep you here on earth with us, it was
wonderful loving you and being loved by you for the time we
had.
We miss you every minute, every day. I feel you close by still.
Rest well our precious daughter.*
    Love,
    Mom

Long after the sunflowers are gone, I'm not feeling well. The CT scan results turn up a few incidental findings of abnormal tissue. During the next two weeks I have two biopsies, a mammogram, an ultrasound, and an MRI. I'm grateful for the speed and short waiting period; ambiguity is challenging.

I don't know how seriously ill people manage through months of tests and uncertainty. I have more compassion and admiration for them now than I ever did before. I tell myself not to worry; after all, the very worst in life has already happened. This health scare is a wake-up call to keep me more alert. While I wait for news, I wonder how Kristina's constant state of anxiety – years of it – felt. I can see now how it wore her down.

Fortunately, I learn from my doctors and biopsy reports that all are non-cancerous. Two outpatient surgeries happen quickly. However, my liver tumor is not operable. I'm referred to a liver specialist and begin a long term care plan.

I call my sister and leave a cell phone message about the good results. She calls back in a few hours. "Trish has a message for you. She said you're very tired and you've got to make a decision. Do you want to live?"

Well, that's harsh, I think to myself.

"Whoa, this is not cancer. No one said anything about dying," I manage to say it slowly. There have been many days when I long to be reunited with Kristina, but I didn't think I was actively attracting illness or death. Slowly I let out a big breath. "Yes, I'll talk with her."

She lets out her own breath. "Good. Now call."

Trish is a practitioner in California who uses guided imagery for health care. I worked with her in the past for post-surgical healing and alternative health techniques.

"How are you feeling?" Trish asks.

"Not great," I tell her. "But I just had good news." That sounds like an illusion. Maybe I haven't learned much about control after all.

"The liver is the seat of anger and frustration. That's not all I'm reading. What I'm getting is rage. Deep rage. You're going to get sicker if you don't get rid of that."

"Really? I've been feeling less anger and calmer," I respond, puzzled.

"It's stored. What you've got to do is release it. It harms your liver."

Trish then guides me in healing imagery. I close my eyes and imagine stomping my feet, eyes shut and arms raised. I feel wild and angry, pulling emotions (from my liver). I send bolts of lightning up through fingertips. It feels like a huge hissy fit for health. I even giggle.

After this healing session I think of Kristina; she always cared for me, always helped whenever I was sick, little deliveries of ginger ale and crackers to the bedside, reading to me from a favorite book. Nothing is the same now. Maybe that's what all my rage was about, inner resistance, still swimming against the grief currents instead of flowing.

55

When I was a teenager living in Pennsylvania my father lost a finger unclogging a snow blower. Ever afterward he would remind us we always have time to think through a problem, even when in a hurry. Don't reach in too soon to fix things. Think it through instead. He shared with us his phantom limb feeling he had afterward, always with him, a finger not really there.

Dad gave Kristina a nickname when she was six months old, Little Pilgrim, after I'd mailed a photo of the three of us dressed in costumes taken at her first Thanksgiving. His death was a few years before Kristina's and I often wished I could talk with him about her loss. I wonder what wise compassionate words he would say about the suicide of his granddaughter. I almost hear his voice, "Losing our Little Pilgrim is like missing my finger; we'll always know she's been here."

56

I don't know why I didn't record Kristina's piano composition. It was a wonderful piano piece. She was taking Suzuki piano lessons. The melody she wrote was joyous, happy and lyric; she called it a "George Winston-type song" that flowed one afternoon while she was practicing. She played it over and over again, committing it to memory, laying down the track as if she were in a recording studio. When we wanted to hear her play it we requested Kristina's Song. Long after she stopped taking piano lessons as a teenager she would sit down at the piano and play her song, never forgot it.

The piano has been in the family for four generations. The black walnut case glows under the brass music light. Double-turned legs with antique brass lyres supported the 1931 Schiller grand, made in Oregon, Illinois. Kristina's fingers were long and firm on the keys. She had an ear for music and with her talent she would have become the best of the family's players. Although I've played that piano for more than fifty years, Kristina brought more passion to her playing. It was a hard decision to drop her instruments, piano and cello, to focus on sports. Through her tears she explained, "I'll come back to it, Mom, once my years as an athlete are over. After all, you kept playing."

Kristina first heard me play when she was a baby. I placed her in an infant seat, nestled it underneath the piano, and played lullabies. Our dog, Bandit, would cuddle up to her, a faithful protector for his baby. Sometimes, even now, I play our favorite songs, Schumann's "Scenes from Childhood," and remember Kristina waving her chubby arms in the air to the music above her, smiling and happy. No one knew then that the piano would one day support funeral flowers and photos from her calling hours. How I would love to hear her play *Kristina's Song* just once more.

57

The telephone is ringing. It's October 2005. On the way to the phone I smile and walk by a sepia pencil portrait of Kristina drawn when she was sixteen. Her likeness turned out incredibly realistic, so like her, with freckles, loose strands of hair and a slight twinkle in her eyes.

"Hello? Mrs. Stahl? It's Dori."

"How's our favorite Philadelphia attorney? And Josh?" Dori is one of Kristina's Colby friends; she's called and emailed to share news about bar exams, new jobs, boyfriends, moves, finding true love, and getting engaged. This call has news too.

"I'm going to be in Connecticut. My mother and I want you to come with us to pick out my wedding dress. Please say you'll come?"

I choke with sudden tears and can't even speak at first. "What a precious invitation. I'm honored."

We settle on the time and place and I hang up the phone. Another wedding, another of Kristina's friends involving us in ways I could never have imagined years ago. I feel genuinely happy for her and grateful to be included on this special occasion to select a wedding gown.

The day we meet, I bring a digital camera, determined to give them a happy photo record of gowns Dori will go through. The sheer number of dresses in the bridal store is amazing. The attendant carefully maneuvers the bride in and out of dresses. The creations lift over her head, hover around Dori's tiny frame, and flutter down as she tries on, at minimum, twenty five dresses. Now I know why they describe them as frothy. After the first ten we get a clearer idea of the dream dress she's looking for – strapless, not too full or too narrow, minimal trim, delicate beading but no sequins, satin, and romantic without being fussy. I am astounded at the vast number of wedding gowns fitting that description.

Dori is quite the trouper while Debby and I wilt nearby on slipper chairs. Thirty photos later, one glorious selection is pulling away from the pack. Do we have a winner? Maybe, but it isn't exactly this one. The bridal salon is telephoning New York to see if a similar gown by the same designer that Dori likes best is available. We'll have to see.

Bill and I have been to twelve weddings now since Kristina died. Although never easy, weddings are journey steps too in healing. We love the young women and men; they are our friends now *because* Kristina died, friends in a way that would not have been possible if she had lived.

On the other hand, funerals remain wicked hard. Impossible to prevent, I know now to expect a vortex to grab me and whirl me around in memories. There hasn't been a funeral or memorial service I've attended since Kristina died when I don't think of hers. It feels very physical when I get whisked back emotionally to that seat in church on the left aisle, the front pew, trying to figure out how I got there to begin with. Imagining your own child's death is not the same as participating in her funeral; my nightmares and worries never came close.

Services bring a visceral déjà vu feeling. As much as I have loved the person whose funeral I'm attending when this happens, I leave my seated body and travel back to that one service, those words about her, our ministers. The music I hear is "Tears in Heaven" and "Bring Her Home" sung at her service. The smells of candles, aged wood, and altar flowers come back full force along with human sounds of coughs, noses being blown, and whispering.

At some point I do eventually return to the physical and emotional reality of where I am, who has died, and the difference between the present day loss and the past. It's not about me; it's always about her.

58

I'm shattering ... and all I did was walk into a gift shop in Tahoe, California. I can't move, can't breathe, can't stop a purse from sliding off my shoulder to hit the stone floor.

My sister and I have been skiing and now we're doing a little off-slope browsing in the nearby shops. What stops me is a little thing, something innocent and normal – a display of Vera Bradley colorful quilted handbags, satchels, and accessories. This brand was Kristina's favorite.

Although we gave her friends almost everything from her collections, I kept one bag, a pattern we picked out together that last visit to Bread Loaf. Her things are still inside from her last day of life – matching Vera Bradley wallet, keys, cosmetic bag, contacts and solution, sunglasses, hair brush, and sugar-free dental chewing gum – ordinary items almost anyone would carry, a small slice of her life, little utilitarian aids organized by Vera Bradley. Now I'm standing in California, less than three feet from a display, and I'm frozen in place, playing back the memory video. Who would have thought grief could attack so suddenly?

"What's the matter?" Ginny comes back to get me and recognizes the grief ambush taking place even though I'm unable to speak. No matter how often it happens, it's a surprise to lose control, even over things that were joyful to our daughter. Grief is bittersweet, intense, making it impossible to move or do anything but experience it flow through.

Two years later, I find myself shopping in another store at home in Connecticut. Plimpton's was a stationery, luggage and gift shop where Kristina often shopped. I'm looking for a gift, hoping to find something fun. The kindly clerk, who also knew Kristina, comes up to me and says, "Your daughter would come here often to look through the new arrivals, spending a half hour sometimes just looking at all the styles. She loved her Vera Bradleys didn't she?"

"Yes, she did. Now I wonder what she'd pick out for her great-aunt in Florida."

I'm pleased I can actually say this. Some sadness creeps up on me as I watch the clerk ring up the sale, a quilted, black and yellow paisley photo holder. The feeling now is softer, a longing for her to be with me to enjoy this shopping. I decide to insert a photo before mailing, one of Kristina hugging her Great-Aunt Ginny.

59

Instead of a near-death experience, suicide creates a post-death feeling for a survivor who has lost a loved one, very similar to an out-of-body sensation. I feel detached sometimes and observe myself going through motions, hear myself having entirely lucid conversations. Life goes on, but on the edge, at the fringe of things, not feeling fully engaged or involved, hovering. I strive to connect with the essence of what Kristina left behind, while at the same time I keep moving. I know what surreal feels like now. It's unnatural, irrational, dreamlike and completely normal after suicide.

60

The lovely colonial home comes into sight around a curve in the road. A quiet neighborhood, a beautiful spring-like day in early December, and an impossible setting for death. Several young people are leaving the house. Others are getting into parked cars, talking quietly and weeping. This grief scene is familiar.

Their dog greets people on the doorstep, her sweet eyes look up to each friend or family member as they stop to pat, feeling comfort themselves from that small loving act. Her tail echoes a soft thump as the door opens and closes. The welcoming kitchen is crowded. Each new arrival is greeted with care. It's warm and cozy in the room. "Tim's not here, but Ellen is somewhere in the kitchen. She'll want to see you," I am told. Just then I see Ellen glance up from a friend's shoulder and I find myself moving to hug her too.

She whispers in our embrace, "One of my first thoughts at the hospital when we got the news was to talk to you and Bill." She takes my hand and we step into the quiet dining room.

"How to go on?" I recognize the plea in her eyes from my own experience as a mother whose child died.

"Your purpose for living must seem lost for now – ours did too," I say. "But you *will* find a way through this. Just not yet. You go on one breath at a time. You'll build a new purpose. In time, all in time." I stop. Too soon for her to take so much in. I advise them to drink lots of water for the dehydrating grief that is now a constant companion. Be gentle. Go slowly, carefully. Reid's grieving parents and his sister are patients, as if they were in intensive care themselves after this trauma that is so great.

"Why? How could this happen?" Ellen asks.

"God didn't plan for this to happen. I don't believe it when people say this is God's plan. God had plans for Reid – for Kristina too – and life happened in a random, tragic way. God is weeping with you now in grief," I answer.

"You know what I'm worried about the most?" I shake my head. "No one in our families has died. There's no one in Heaven to greet Reid. He's alone."

"He was never alone, not during the car accident, not afterward. Ellen, what time did Reid die?"

"They lost him once, just after the accident, but they got him back. Then at Hartford Hospital, during surgery, his heart stopped again. They couldn't get him back. It was maybe 3:00 a.m. when the surgeon came into the waiting room. I saw his face ... and I knew."

I absorb her story, picturing the hours after getting the news, waiting, reaching Tim in Baltimore, his drive home, praying, talking, holding each other through the hours. Her story makes me think about what happened to me last night.

About 2:45 or 3:00 a.m. I woke up with a feeling of alertness. Sometimes I feel Kristina's spirit reaching me and this was that kind of feeling. A little wake-up-call by her spirit coming to me. There was no sense of urgency, yet it was a compelling feeling. I decided to get out of bed and go into the family room where I sat by the fireplace. I wrapped myself in the prayer shawl Ellen knit me when Kristina died. As always, it both warmed and comforted me.

So I sat there in the quiet and heard Kristina's sweet gentle voice in my head, *It's all right, Mom. Everything's fine. Tell her he's all right.*

Since I wasn't troubled or disquieted about any problems or thoughts, I didn't understand what she meant. She didn't sound unhappy or distressed. It was a peaceful reassurance meant to comfort, but clearly the message was not meant for me. So I went back to bed pondering one of life's little mysteries that I accept and know will take time to figure out.

The next morning we had an early telephone call from our minister letting us know about the tragedy, that Reid was killed in an automobile accident. Two friends were passengers. The passengers will survive. Before going to the Hollister's home I first wrote a letter to Kristina:

Dear Kristina,
I don't know how these things work in Heaven, but please embrace a new soul who has joined you, Reid Hollister. You may

have met him at church or school where he was a student too. He was in a car accident. It happened so fast. He didn't want to leave here. He is young, afraid. You know how that was. Please help him find his peace and his new place in God's home.

    Love,

    Mom

"People always say he's in a better place. It's just another place. I happen to think a better place is here with us," Ellen says.

"Ellen, you and Tim may not have family members in heaven yet, but Reid did have someone to greet and love him into heaven. Kristina wants me to give you a message. Reid is fine, in a safe loving place. All is well with your son."

61

I've come to New York to attend the performance of Vanessa Redgrave in *The Year of Magical Thinking*, the one-woman play based on Joan Didion's memoir, one of my favorite grief journey books. One of two friends with me, Judy, also lost a daughter to suicide. We met when a mutual friend asked us to help Judy and Jerry those first horrific days. We help each other and that includes going to this play.

Linda Finkler, a long-time friend who visited me in the hospital the day after Kristina was born, is seated to my left. She opened her home as "Camp Finkler" for Kristina with her two boys in the summer when day care was not in session. We have a deep personal history together, a rich friendship.

The three of us are seated in the fourth row. The audience at the matinee is predominantly women. From the many aged faces, I imagine some may have lost a child. A few, like me, carry a copy of Didion's book. In it Didion wrote about how tragedy arrives on otherwise ordinary days, the vortex.

There was nothing ordinary about the day our Kristina died. One year after the United States was attacked by terrorists there were services of remembrance broadcasting on most channels. Church bells rang. Televisions were brought in to workplaces and we had a commemorative lunch together at Kaiser, honoring the 9/11 dead. The mood around that time may have added to Kristina's depression. We'll never know.

I met my own vortex the day of her death, the swirling terror, a suck-back movement of vertigo and nausea. It revisits sometimes. I've come to fear that whirlpool, the drowning feeling. I'm certain now Kristina feared her vortex too.

62

The rectangular box is tucked away, narrow and pristine white even after all these years, resting high on a guest room closet shelf. As I lift it, there's hardly any weight, just shape. My hands shake and I worry about dropping the box and its fragile contents.

I carry the box to one of the antique beds crafted in the 1800s by an Arnold relative on my mother's Scots side of the family. The Poppa bed is long and narrow, the Momma bed short and wide to fit a baby too, and there's a rope-laced trundle bed that slides out from underneath.

A small night stand separates the two beds and across the room is a matching dresser, all the pieces handed down to daughters in the family along with a quilt collection, a legacy of family I'd always intended to pass along to Kristina. When she was first born I nursed her in the Momma bed at night, imagining how the many mothers in my family had done the same thing, savoring warm sleepy baby smells, feeling safe and loved.

The box lid comes off easily. Inside, the tissue paper looks fresh, undamaged after twenty six years. I part the edges gently, opening to a small white embroidered christening gown, complete with tiny cap and sleeveless under-slip. Tears come and I pause to breathe in, breathe out. Hard to believe our daughter was once that little. Bill's mother bought the christening gown as a gift and embroidered Kristina's name on the hem. I trace her neat even stitches with my fingers – *Kristina Ann Stahl, June 2, 1977*. Bill and I were thrilled at her birth and imagined more babies' names joining their sister's on the gown, eventually handing it down as a family heirloom with the furniture.

I lift the sheer garments out and shake them gently to unfurl delicate embroidered cotton. There are minuscule tucks, flowers and decorative knots. The cap is darling, a tiny bonnet of artistry and long ribbons. I smile and remember how baby Kristina kept working it off, intent on removing it every time we tried to reposition it before the baptism. Eventually we gave up and let her gum the ribbons. She rewarded us with smiles and coos, seeming to enjoy the service, the two other babies, all the new faces and eager arms to hold her that day.

The reason I'm here going through this box is because I have an idea, something small to remember her by with her friends, now having babies themselves. I'm going to embroider all their babies' names around the hem; whether they use the gown or not. I want to do this for me. They've become our extended family now.

I locate the old family embroidery needles, kept in an ancient wooden box, handed down with the quilts. I'll buy all different colors of floss, silken and shiny, then make little chain stitches in flowing script, careful not to pull too tight. *This is something I can do*, I think.

How I wish I could stitch our lives back together as easily, mend the brokenness, rip out any mistakes and re-stitch those, restore our family. Snip, snip and pull out her suicide. Knot new thread. Over-stitch the damage. Reconnect life threads.

63

I am uneasy venturing into the restaurant. The last time I was here, our book club had met for dinner and discussion of Maya Angelou's book *I Know Why the Caged Bird Sings*.

That dinner had been very special; Kristina was our guest facilitator for the conversation. She sent us pre-reading, prepared questions, and identified linkages with many of the author's other works. She loved getting us to talk about the book and encouraged personal insights and connections. Many of the book club women are mothers of Kristina's school friends.

We delighted in her poise and preparation, the way she managed the discussion, the skill she brought to the table from her studies in African-American literature. We all learned from her. Not for one minute did she appear uncomfortable or anxious. Maybe she kept her mask of achievement and self confidence on that night too? It's frustrating that my memory holds no answers. The mystery wins again.

64

Five years after Kristina's death and I'm still watching for her. I look to the street, willing a black Jeep to pull in with our daughter at the wheel, waving hello as she parks. Her dark ponytail swinging behind her, I see her walk across the gravel drive, come to the front door. We drive past her condo several times in the normal course of a day. I used to be able to see the sliding doors of her living room off the patio visible from the street, and I would glance to the second floor bedroom, imagining her moving around. When she was living close to us, I rejoiced to see lights on, thinking she was in her home, safe and sound. Now when I drive by, the unit is obscured by dense wooded growth and the lights are rarely on. Yet, I look over every time, every drive-by.

When we're on the Colby College campus in Maine I expect to see her there too, especially among the soccer and lacrosse players. I imagine her competing in the games, her left foot sending soccer balls flying, or watching her sprint down the lacrosse field, cradling a ball in her basket, turning defense into offense. I superimpose her laughing face onto a dark-haired player who laughs and hugs teammates after victory, just like Kristina would. As we drive by the house where she lived in Waterville her senior year, I strain to see if it's her standing in the driveway waving to a passing car, standing exactly the same way she did so many times when we pulled away after a visit. It seems the Maine air prompts visions and memories we have of Kristina enjoying the happiest years of her life.

At night I listen for sounds from her former bedroom above ours, convinced I hear a shoe fall, soft music, a murmur as she talks on the phone, the shower running, even the slight creaking of her bed as she settles down or rolls over. Compelled, I tiptoe up the stairs, open the

153

door and look in to see if all is well. It's not as if I rationally expect to see her again. I simply stay open to any opportunity to reconnect and be present with her spirit once again.

65

Soft lighting turns the private dining room into an intimate haven. We see the snowy February landscape and winter garden just outside draped windows as we gather together for the last evening of our memoir writing class. Six women sit at the round table, lingering over every bite and sip of tea, reluctant to end our time together. We've become friends during this week-long program held at the Mayflower Inn & Spa in Connecticut.

It's been an intense experience for me, an impossible one without our writing teacher, Dani Shapiro, a best-selling author and the heart of our small group of writers. Her firm and gentle handling has directed and supported our efforts. We trust her as well as value her guidance. We bloom, we thrive, and our writing improves.

Each night after dinner we have readings. Dani gives the first reading from *Black & White*, one of her novels. We gather by the fireplace in the gracious living room. We're from Boston, Denver, Washington D.C., New York and two small towns in Connecticut. We range in age from thirty to sixty, here to learn a new genre. The windows rattle a bit with winter gusts and the fire crackles every now and then. Perfect storytelling atmosphere. Dani begins reading, drawing us into a New York world of photography, mothers and daughters, engaging us with vivid words and images.

This last night it's my turn to read from the memoir I'm working on. Dani bolsters my confidence simply by sitting beside me. I face the others, eager for their feedback. Then I read; my voice chokes with emotion. I make eye contact occasionally but mostly stay focused on getting through words that hardly seem my own. There is a hush afterward, then sniffles and sighs.

"You didn't see their faces while you were reading," Dani says. "But I did. They were right there, experiencing everything with you."

We took Kristina's presence in our lives for granted, believing she would continue to be with all of us for years. I drank in her laughter, warmth and goodness as a matter of course. I thought we were normal, never once realizing how greatly we were blessed. Maybe I'm even changing the past unknowingly when I write? I question whether she was really as wonderful a child and adult as I remember. A pragmatic realistic person in the "before," I suspect I've morphed into more of a sentimentalist in the "after."

66

Sacred places, big or little shrines, calm me. Walking in a cemetery soothes me; I don't fear places for the dead. What I feel is appreciation for the people buried, people who had meaningful lives, family and friends. I take note of the mourners and caretakers who walk in the spaces with me. These people are like me, left behind. There are rows of graves, occasional monuments, one or two mausoleums.

I'm also drawn to churches, synagogues, retreat chapels, war memorials, and garden alcoves that shelter stones and statues. The sacredness feels tangible. Funny, but I can't remember how I felt before. Respect, certainly, but not a deep resonance of connection that I feel now in these places. Death did that for me, opening a path for reflection and meditation, solace found in the sacred.

There is a large labyrinth inside an open hall of our church patterned after the labyrinth installed around 1220 CE in the cathedral of Chartres, France. At the center is a rosette, a six-petal rose that is a symbol of both divine and human love. I had never walked a labyrinth before Kristina died, wasn't even aware of the difference between a labyrinth and a maze, and so I walk tentatively, appreciating all the twists and turns, like my own life.

A maze was designed to confound the mind; a labyrinth gives mental release. I feel certain walking a labyrinth would have helped Kristina, a therapeutic action to give her respite from the brain chemistry wreaking havoc with her life. For me, beaten up by regret and self-blame, I feel better after walking the path, physically settled. I find peace there and surrender to winding and unwinding my own mind.

67

A happy dream wakes me one morning. In it, Bill is making breakfast for Kristina before taking her to day care, when she's only four or five years old. Cheery little-girl sounds come from our blue and white kitchen. I pause at the door, hesitant, not wanting to intrude on their time together.

Bill has his eye on eggs he's cooking in a frying pan on the stove top. He's got a spatula in his right hand. The kitchen is exactly the same in the dream as in real life with warm, cherry wood cabinets. On the opposite side of one counter there's a round dining table where Kristina is seated. She's perched on a phone book on the chair. She's singing along with her Daddy to a song from "Annie." *The sun will come out tomorrow, tomorrow ... just a day away.*

She sees me. "Mommy!" Arms raise, both little hands wave, and she gives me a bright smile. She points down at her plate. "Look what Daddy fixed me." I walk over to her.

"Look ... look!" Kristina reaches out to me, holds my hand and shows me her plate. There I see a smile made from a banana, raisin eyes, and apple slice ears – her personal food smiley face to start the day. I bend over and give her a hug, filled with little girl happiness.

"Daddy says you make the best fruit animals. But, HE makes the best faces!" She's so happy.

When I wake up from this dream I look around the room but I don't start crying. I hug the visitation and savor it.

68

The last Christmas all three of us were together was in 2001. Kristina gave us a pastel she'd drawn and framed, one with strong colors and movement, a vibrant circle with swirls of yellow, gold orange, red, and black, radiating out or moving in, depending on the viewer's perspective. The outer edge of black is dense and hovering, but not overtly threatening, just *there*, a presence, seemingly in balance with the rest of the composition. There's a stunning glowing yellow core, set slightly to the left side of the canvas.

Her art made me think of a photograph I'd seen from the Hubbard telescope series, a glorious reminder from deep space of mystery and energy, beauty and force. Her art gift had power too, as if it could throb out to us. We asked her when she started pastels and how she'd learned. She laughed with delight.

"Lately I've wanted to draw circles, this theme over and over. Kind of abstract, using different colors. Chris is getting one too," she told us.

"Is the light pushing back the dark or is the dark trying to take over the light?" I asked.

"What do you think?" she asks. Like most artists she was making us work at interpreting it for ourselves.

"Both," I say.

"Dad, what do you think?" Kristina asked.

Bill had tears in his eyes and pulled her to him in a big hug. "You are so generous. This is wonderful! Thank you, sweetie."

Now, when I look at the painting seven years later, I see the darkness and drawing circles repetitively as other clues we missed. Maybe in a way she was trying to express the mental spiraling she endured? The black looks menacing now, advancing, not pushed back by the light and color at all.

When I found her art things at the condo, I looked at all the completed acrylics, water colors and pastels she'd stored in a large portfolio holder. One pad of paper, the same 20" x 24" size she'd given us, held ten more circular compositions, very similar, but with different colors. Sometimes there was no black. Did she repeat the theme as practice? Or was this another clue of obsessive-compulsive behavior, trying to get it right?

The problem with suicide is you go back and re-frame everything. It could have been innocent practice painting to test different colors and effects, preliminary sketches, learning her way as an artist, not necessarily OCD manifesting. Now, I taint it all with the perspective of suicide. It saddens me that one legacy of her death is that I even think these things, that I try to second-guess what was going on, imagining a mental state in a way that would never have occurred to me before. "After" means I'm filtering through a suicide lens.

69

While trying to solve the mystery of suicide, I feel myself changing. I rediscover things I used to enjoy, that somehow slipped away from me, and now bring meaning to my life once again. The critical voice in my head is still strong, however, probably similar to the one Kristina listened to in hers. It keeps at me to do something, be something. It is taking real discipline to break out of my head and stay in the moment. Although it feels good, it's a deliberate conscious practice to become mindful; things as simple as feeling the cold, taking walks, seeing friends, telephoning family more often, even tasting food I've cooked; all have to be consciously done to keep my thoughts from moving away into grief.

I miss my body the most. Funny thought, that, since there is more of me now than before her death. What I liked about the "before" body was being strong and healthy from exercise, the one that responded to hills and valleys when jogging and let me sleep at night. That body didn't crave comfort food like a drug to numb the pain.

All of this taking stock doesn't come easily for me. Work had consumed so much time before. In a way, I recognize what performance anxiety did to our daughter; I painfully and regretfully see the role I had in passing on to her that constant striving for achievement, as if simply being ourselves was not enough for either of us.

An important insight I gained from reflection and discussion in counseling is that Kristina's anxiety, practically full-blown terror toward the end, was about being alone, feeling isolated even amidst many friends, colleagues and family. A private person normally, the social distancing might not have felt too uncomfortable to Kristina at first. Athletes live in groups of people, have binding social relationships with each other and coaches. Kristina lived in her own place after graduation, but she never felt entirely comfortable, not as she did when in the dorm and at school with a team support system and coaches around her. As her illness deepened, she was increasingly isolated, afraid. Standing up in front of students and teaching must have become agony. Her lower intestinal system rebelled regularly, forcing her to rush to the rest room. Physical and emotional symptoms were there, yet we missed them.

So, I'm looking back, trying to find my way forward. Bill and I know our counseling sessions are very valuable to rebuild our lives, and that means tearing down, clearing out, and making space for the new as well. A recurring topic is how to deal with not seeing Kristina grow up and have children. We didn't realize how much we were looking forward to enjoying our daughter as a mother, being grandparents; we were lulled into thinking we'd be together for decades, moving into a whole new generation. By contrast, the new normal is irrevocably empty, looming without the usual family milestones.

In order to understand Kristina's suicide, I've also searched my own past to find a similar time when I felt alone, unable to keep going on, afraid and at a loss. The closest I can come was in 1972. Bill and I had been married for a year and he received orders for an unaccompanied tour to South Korea. We were relieved he wasn't posted to Vietnam, and I made arrangements to work as a teacher for a small Methodist Board of Missions school in Wonju, South Korea, near the base shared by the Republic of Korea's Army, the US Army and the US Air Force. I arrived in November and lived on the mission compound, close to a regional hospital about two miles from the military base.

While in South Korea, Bill was posted on a temporary assignment to Vietnam. He received a phone call at dinner, went upstairs to pack, and off he went to the base for transport. I remember feeling out-of-control, yet I was doing things in an orderly way. I walked with Bill to the helicopter pad; we hugged and kissed good-bye. And then he lifted off into the air, banking right past a rice paddy field on the edge of the landing pad.

In shock, I walked to the base cafeteria for coffee with some of his Air Force buddies. I heard their bracing words, "Think of this as an inconvenience, something you'll get through." I was too numb to feel much, but what sank in was the thought that it would end, we'd get through it.

For months I kept the mantra going in my heart and head – *this is inconvenient but it will end.* By then the military surge of the TET offensive was in the news every day. Wonju was active and tense as more military were deployed. Two other wives who were living off base like me went home instead of waiting it out. Then the small Methodist school where I worked closed and the missionaries went home. I remember seeing them off on the train with my Korean friends gathered to say goodbye. They assured me I could continue to rent the house until Bill returned.

I had lost my husband temporarily to war, our military friends were scattered, and my job ended. Alone in a foreign country where I spoke only a few words of the language, I felt alone at age twenty two and considered going back home without Bill. Then a mobile army remote call from him in Vietnam kept me there. He'd managed a few minutes to connect and reassure me he was all right. So, I decided to stay and volunteer at the Chechon Children's Orphanage. As time went by I lost weight, hovering around a hundred pounds, feeling listless.

Early one afternoon, I heard a knock on the door and a soft voice, "Karin? It's Father Ernie." I hurried to let in Father Ernest Sullivan, Catholic missionary priest serving in Wonju. We had all become friends through one of the Army families who'd left. Father Ernie was my lifeline that day, very patient and calm. I'm sure he sensed I was at a breaking point, exhausted, alone, and depleted.

"We priests all have little breakdowns over here. Missionary work is hard. You know you're close to having one now, don't you?"

It was a relief to hear him say it, to identify my distress. People recover. I'll survive too. This can be fixed. The first step was dinner, so I made us some food and felt better dining with company for a change. I had many questions for him about what I should do or if I needed to see a doctor. Not once did I think I was suicidal; yet I might have been if left alone any longer.

His insight and compassion in that remote mountain village in South Korea brought strength and grounded me. He helped me get a grip and stabilize. I would not have reached out; I simply couldn't. My fears, diminished health, and feelings of isolation overwhelmed me. I didn't know what was happening, but he did. I understand this crisis in my life now in a way I wouldn't have if Kristina hadn't died. I had a savior in Father Ernie, someone who recognized I needed help and was willing to support me.

So, if I'd had this experience in my own past, why didn't I recognize what was happening to Kristina?! Why couldn't I do for her what Father Ernie did for me?

After Bill ended his tour in Vietnam and we both returned home to the States, I buried this memory. I didn't think of this time until after Kristina died. I have no way of understanding why I didn't make the connection, remember my own trauma, and get her help – be her Father Ernie. The despair I felt must have been similar to hers, lethal things happening at the same time. I had help with the tunnel vision; she went through it alone. Father Ernie gave me a gift of feeling safe, helped me choose to not give up, and gave me *another option*. I blame myself for not doing the same for Kristina.

Kristina chose to find a safe place for herself beyond life. I understand some of the mystery now; her need for safety overrode the violence of causing her own death. No one wants to die alone, even her. That's why she made two phone calls, one to us and then the last one to Chris. She wanted to hear our voices and connect one last time, know we loved her before she left this world. I think she wrote her good-bye note before calling us September 10, 2002.

For years I reread her good-bye letter. I read with my head for the longest time, not knowing how to embrace all she wrote with her heart. The trouble she thought she caused, feeling a failure, seeking a safe place, worrying about what would happen afterward, hating herself, feeling shame, wanting forgiveness – huge emotional distress she could not overcome alone. It was impossible to overcome when she felt so hopeless, helpless and exhausted. There is little mystery to understand now, just painful acceptance.

Since my daughter's death, I feel an urge to go back and do everything over, getting it right this time. The search for clues to Kristina's state of mind has revealed there was a complex linking of events, all moving toward a fatal convergence with everything going wrong at the same time. If I got a do-over I'd pick a day, hour, or minute when I could make a difference to save her life.

Specialists tell me I wouldn't be anguishing this much over her death if she had been hit by a car or had a disease. The fact she died by suicide, that I'm left behind as a survivor, is what makes accepting her death different. Our daughter's choice to leave this world was irrational; it was the dis-ease with herself caused by the disease in her mind. She was seriously ill, her brain chemistry out of balance, with no rational thinking and resiliency. This I understand from clinical explanations. It also makes my heart ache. With her anxiety condition she couldn't see a less fierce reality, one where making a life or death choice wasn't necessary, and one where grey is normal.

Our daughter's genetic makeup and mental hard wiring set her on a path. One grandmother self-medicated for anxiety, another attempted suicide when severely depressed. Kristina saw me go through work stress many times. It was no surprise she drove herself to achieve in sports and academics, worried about being good enough, afraid to make mistakes, aware others depended on her as a leader.

According to one study I read, shame is one of our earliest childhood feelings after a failure. Our daughter wrote in her anxiety workbook that she was "taught" her anxiety. The lesson she learned is not to fail in order to avoid shame. Unfortunately, the mental re-framing she did increased the level of her shame feelings.

"My bad" is an expression people sometimes use as a way of admitting error. It has a quick, don't-make-this-a-federal-case nuance to it. It's a way of owning the problem, apologizing; it means I recognize I am responsible and I'm sorry. It also diminishes any sense of shame, a healthy direction to get over mistakes without more damage. Imagine if we all quickly acknowledged mistakes without taking on shame? What a relief that would have been for Kristina too.

The yearning to right a mistake comes from deep in our hearts. Sadly, there are no second chances for some things. Futures are destroyed. People die. Children take their own lives. Disasters happen. The world shifts. Sometimes it *is* too late and we can't make it right. Nevertheless, we feel compelled to do something, to learn from our mistakes. We strain to go forward, do better the next time.

As humans we are works in progress; we hope for improvement. To replace our doubt with certainty, even when it seems the magnitude of a mistake is too great, we hope and believe a do-over will set our world right. The Twelve Step programs of recovery all include making amends and forms of do-over. The step requires practice and strengthens people, rebuilding their futures.

"There is always the option," Kristina wrote.

That was code for knowing that if all else failed, suicide was a choice. In her world there was no do-over. She punished herself for not measuring up to what she thought others expected of her and what she expected of herself as a teacher. She came to believe there is no way to correct mistakes, no second chances, no forgiveness for normal minor errors in judgment or action. Her mistakes seemed immense in her mind and she felt immobilized, close to spinning out of control. Suicidal ideation blows imagined mistakes out of proportion; the person becomes convinced there is no way out of the dilemma. It is that kind of thinking that defeats.

There is no do-over for me to save her life. However, I now have knowledge to help recognize someone in crisis or who feels suicidal. *I have options.* I can reach out without hesitancy, not worry about myself or what they'll think. If I'm wrong, that's fine. They'll know I cared. It's a way of living that second chance, to get it right this time for someone else.

70

When another Kristina dream comes, I'm gripped with its intensity. I feel immersed in the sharp images, so realistic. Her forehead has damp little curls plastered onto skin beaded with sweat. Her cheeks are bright red, stretched tight with fever burning inside her small, four-year old body. Her nightgown needs to be changed again. It's time for another baby aspirin, fluids, and temperature check. Her normally bright blue eyes are dull, her lids heavy with sickness and exhaustion. This is an awful case of the flu. I see her focus on my face. She tries a little smile, quivers with the effort.

"Hi sweetie," I say. "It's time for some more to drink and an aspirin." I put my arm around her back and lift as gently as possible. She moans a little, feels limp. I rearrange the pillows to prop her up.

"Mommy, I hurt," she whispers.

"I know, honey. It's the flu. You'll feel better in a while. Here's your aspirin, Pumpkin." I brush back the sticky hair from her brow and bring the water glass and straw to her lips, gently putting the aspirin inside her mouth.

"Drink as much water as you can. Lots and lots."

Kristina sips and then gulps. After half a glass she shakes her head and croaks, "No more."

I help ease her back onto the pillows, feeling completely powerless as I gaze on her flushed face. So vulnerable. Almost a third of our elementary school children are ill, including many teachers, and several schools closed for a week to reduce spreading the flu. Bill and I are by Kristina's bedside around the clock, watching carefully for signs of dehydration and other indications she may need hospitalization. In Connecticut, two children have died from this flu already.

167

Kristina's small shoulders shake when I pick her up to take her to the bathroom. I feel her slipping away as I walk, disappearing from my arms. When I wake up I'm holding my arms out, empty.

71

Early, in the hard grieving, I put a little bit of Kristina's belongings everywhere, scattering them throughout the house, in our cars, outside in the yard, in her friends' homes. The idea was to have her continue to be present in our lives in useful, normal ways. Little jars of spices, packaged for singles who don't cook often, joined mine in the kitchen cupboard. I like reaching for spices and see hers intermingled with ours on the shelf. Each time I use rosemary, dill or garlic I may shake and sometimes drop the tiny servings, but she's there and that means something.

Cleaning products find their way into my hands, brands I didn't use but *she* had. I try her toiletries, dry my hair holding her blower, exercise in her gym clothes – anything and everything becomes part of my life now. Touching them comforts me.

Kristina's things occupy our rooms, drawers and closets around the house; it is easy to weave her into the fabric of our lives in this after time. Lotion and candle scents fill the air. Music from her CDs replaces the sound of her voice. Collapsible lawn chairs, cushions for bleachers, travel mugs for beverages, ponchos and jackets, and all her sports paraphernalia simply continue to serve purpose, different users.

Now after ten years, many of her things are worn out or used up. When something dwindles with last drops clinging to bottle sides, I feel emotional as I try to wring out the last tiny bit. I discard bottles and tubes, each one touched by her, impossible to replace. Who would have thought shampoo could feel sacred. As I surrender her finished things to the wastebasket I feel gratitude. Products weren't important to her, people were.

72

The morning of September 11, 2002, her death had occurred already and I wasn't aware. Isn't there supposed to be a Mommy Radar that sends a signal immediately when your child is at risk or dies? I didn't receive any signals, not even a twinge. Our most precious gift, a child, had passed without my awareness, a tragedy and loss so deep, yet I didn't feel her passing. How could that be? One morning I woke up and didn't know our daughter was no longer in this world. Now, her absence is constant, like her presence used to be.

I brave one question over and over in counseling, "Could I have saved our daughter's life?" The extremely difficult answer to accept is we'll never know. Kristina wore a mask to protect us from the depth and terror of her feelings. She gave off few clues about her distress, considered her panic attacks evidence of weakness. The hopelessness, helplessness and isolation she felt prevented her from reaching for help at the end. She didn't see any way out. Suicide appeared to be the only option left. Was it up to me to reach out before the line was crossed and the suicide impulse became irreversible? I feel very strongly that the answer to this question is yes. But I missed the signs, missed the opportunity to save her life. It took her death to make me aware.

73

It's another December. The snow falls softly, slowly and gently, accumulating on the gravel drive, in the woods, and on the tree branches. Sound is muffled.

I've just finished folding a Christmas sweater, one I get out each year, thinking with optimism that I might feel cheery enough to wear it. I still haven't worn it since the "before" time, captured in a photo taken Christmas day at a friend's house with us – Bill, Kristina and me – in front of their tree. Our friends had adopted a baby girl that long ago Christmas-sweater year. Now, years later, the grown daughter suffers from bipolar disorder.

No family is immune to mental illness or tragedy. We help each other do the best we can to journey through the pain, reassuring ourselves we are not alone and our children can be helped. We share articles, advice from televised programs, Internet sites with information, and guidance. We share our lives in conversation and support each other wherever, and however, we can. We simply carry on.

74

Several years after Kristina's death, I experience search dreams. These are very different from the rescue dreams; not at all distressing, although I never actually see her.

I go on adventures, travel to foreign countries, climb mountains, scuba dive into submerged wrecks, walk miles of beaches, fly planes, follow trails, and meet people everywhere. Many assure me they've seen Kristina and will take me to her. In these dreams I arrive in places where I've never been, jungles and deserts, yet I'm there, believing reports that she is still among us. I go about the trips happily. I have no doubts that I'll catch up to her.

The End

After

Suicide draws a line between "before" and "after" deeply and permanently. Fortunately, there are wonderful national, regional, and local resources for the prevention of suicide and support for survivors. My starting point is always the American Foundation for Suicide Prevention, www.afsp.org

When I'm asked to speak about lessons and insights, I remember how unaware I was before our daughter's suicide, how lacking in knowledge about the complexity and depth of her mental illness.

Suicide prevention:
- Be aware. Be fully present in the moment.
- When you're having conversations with your children, clues and hints to their mental states are subtle, hard to detect, masked. Trust your instinct if something feels wrong.
- Help your children find their own voice. They struggle to grow and articulate their feelings. Model this by speaking in your own voice, your true self, honestly and openly. Show your child it's safe to speak about feelings and fears.
- "There is nothing perfect. There is only life." This is one of my favorite quotes by Sue Monk Kidd from her book *The Secret Life of Bees*. It is incredibly useful and life-saving to really believe this always. Make sure your children know you are not perfect; they'll accept imperfection in themselves more readily when they're convinced that's the normal way of life.
- Learn as much as possible about your family's mental health, not just physical health, history. Inform your children at an appropriate age and involve them in their own health. None of this is their "fault" and needs to become part of their self-management plan for the rest of their lives in some cases. Give them the gift of health history knowledge.
- If a child is adopted, find out about the birth parents' family health history. Anxiety, depression, bi-polar conditions, mood disorders, substance dependence – this hardwiring predisposes us and our children.
- DNA testing is making phenomenal strides in mapping out health issues to address with potential treatment. As more tests become available, the future will bring mental illness markers. Utilize DNA resources.
- Seek early treatment for all mental health needs. Diagnosis and ongoing care are the very best tools for our silent warriors.
- If financial constraints hold you back, push harder for federal, state, and community-funded resources for your child. Taxes are being paid to help children and young adults; find those resources and keep up treatment.
- Welcome children to share their writing with you, even reading out loud personal journal entries, stories, and poems. Our daughter wrote what she couldn't speak about her worsening condition.

- Be particularly proactive about bullying, including text and cyber forms. Bullying about personal characteristics, gender, sexuality, and personality, will damage and put children at risk if not addressed by schools, parents and the community.

- With bullying, both sides suffer and need help. Give treatment and guidance to the bully, as well as to the victim.

- At school, empower children by providing a safe place for everyone.

- Share your faith and beliefs. What gives you hope and strength? Where do you find courage? Your example strengthens your child when they experience their own dark nights of the soul and need to find their way.

- Discuss really tough topics and questions about life. How can we serve the world? What will the future of our country be? What shall I work at? What is my passion in life that makes me happy? Develop a child's skill to generate positive choices.

- Prevent suicide by eliminating it as an option. Recognize and get help for feelings of hopelessness, helplessness, or isolation.

- The support we've received from friends, family, professionals, and even strangers has made all the difference in our healing. Be blessings for those in pain; you may be their solution.

Post-Suicide:
Many individuals and families find becoming active in organizations, schools, and programs serves others as well as themselves. There are many wonderful examples online. Our family and friends found purpose in a few initiatives that honored our daughter:

- Institute of Living Anxiety Disorders Center, Hartford, CT. Kristina Stahl Anxiety Lecture Series for providers, clinical researchers and mental health professionals. Early intervention and treatment make a great difference. Please see www.instituteofliving.org/locations/anxiety-disorders-center

- Colby College, Waterville, ME. Kristina Stahl Creative Writing Fund: Writer-in-Residence, Internships, annual Prize for Creative Nonfiction. www.colby.edu/cwriting/kristina-stahl-creative-writing-fund

- Kingswood Oxford School, West Hartford, CT. Stahl's Sprint for the Teacher Development Fund. www.kingswoodoxford.org

Acknowledgments

Thank you, Kristina Stahl, our daughter, for being the light in our lives as long as was possible for you. Thank you, Bill Stahl, for being a loving supportive husband and a wonderful father. This is your story too.

Thank you, Dani Shapiro, my writing teacher and mentor. I am deeply grateful for your guidance and for the memoir writing programs at the Mayflower Inn and Spa, Sirenland Writers' Conference, and Wishing Stone Workshop. You are a gift and blessing to writers and readers everywhere.

Thank you, Hannah Tinti, for One Story classes for writers and your teaching at Sirenland and Wishing Stone. My thanks to Susan Orlean, Michael Maren, Jim Shepard and fellow workshop writers for your Sirenland strength to write about suicide.

Bill and I thank the Colby College Creative Writing Department in Waterville, Maine, Jennifer Finney Boylan, Debra Spark, and the many writers awarded the Kristina Stahl Writer-in-Residence. You honor Kristina's memory and inspire hundreds of writers. Jenny and Debra, you have made me a better writer.

Thank you Dr. Hank Schwartz, Dr. David Tolin and Susan Dana at The Institute of Living Anxiety Disorders Center. Your expertise and launch of the Kristina Stahl Anxiety Lectures have been invaluable.

Many terrific writer friends and readers have been generous with their time, feedback and compassion over the years. Thank you, D. D. Wood, Irene Levin Berman, Mira Bartok, Bridie Clark, Patrick Tobin, Pam O'Brien, Helen Savage, and Anne-Claude Cotty.

Thank you, Rhonda Mitchell, design consultant, editor, marketing advisor and friend for your awesome publishing talent and wisdom. Thanks to John Beck, the wonderful artist of the sunflower book cover, originally donated for the 2004 Stahl's Sprint fundraiser.

Most of all, I thank my husband, Bill Stahl, sister, Ginny Barrett, brother, Rolf Arentzen, Jr., and our families who encouraged and supported my writing. Blessings to all.

About the Author

Karin Stahl is a communications consultant with The Prescott Group. She is the editor for *Silent Warrior: Finding Voice After Suicide*, and previously published in *Boar's Head Revisited*, *Hartford Courant*, and *Norwegian American*. Her writing programs include Mayflower Memoir Writing, Sirenland Writers' Conference, Wishing Stone Workshop, and One Story Craft Intensive. She lives with her husband in Bloomfield, Connecticut.

Made in the USA
Middletown, DE
02 May 2019